CONSTRAINTS IN DEVELOPMENT OF MANIPUR

Editors

C. Joshua Thomas
R. Gopalakrishnan
R.K. Ranjan Singh

Regency Publications
New Delhi

ISBN 81-87498-30-7

Published by Regency Publications, 20/36–G, Old Market, West Patel Nagar, New Delhi 110 008 for Policy Alternatives for the North-East and Conflict Elimination Awareness (PANACEA), Shillong, and Printed at Radiant Printers, New Delhi 110 008, Phones: 571 2539, 574 0038; Telefax: 578 3571.

Email: regency@satyam.net.in

Preface

A two-day Seminar on "Constraints in the Development of Manipur" sponsored by the Ministry of Home Affairs, Government of India was organised by the Policy Alternatives for North East and Conflict Elimination Awareness (PANACEA) Shillong, North Eastern Regional Centre of the Indian Council of Social Science Research (ICSSR-NERC), and the Manipur Association for Science and Society (MASS) Imphal at the State Guest House Conference Hall, Sanjenthong, Imphal, Manipur during October 18–19, 2000.

Professor Gangmumei Kamei, Hon'ble Minister of Forest and Environment and Law, Government of Manipur, inaugurated the Seminar on 18th October 2000 as Chief Guest. Former Director of Education, Government of Manipur who is at present President of MASS, Imphal, Shri Elangbam Yaima Singh presided over the inaugural function. Smt. M.K. Binodini Devi, Padmashree, a renown writer and women's activist and Lt. General T.S. Shergill, 3 Corp. Commander graced the function as Guests of Honour. Lt. General Shergill rushed to Imphal from Dimapur to attend the Seminar.

The Seminar had five technical sessions in which 15 research papers were presented and discussed. The papers presented by resource persons who include economists, academicians, journalists, environmentalists and social activists deal in various topics in different fields like insurgency, population explosion, ethnic clash, language, impediments in industrial development, law and order, unemployment and status of women in Manipur which are in one way or another are constraints in the development of Manipur. After the deliberations it adopted six resolutions which are being recommended to the Government of Manipur.

Earlier, inaugurating the Seminar, the Hon'ble Minister of Forests and Environment and Law, Professor Gangmumei Kamei stressed the need for restoration of peace and normalcy to step up the pace of development in the state. He said, without peace there can not be development. Describing the Seminar as very timely, the Hon'ble Minister expressed the hope that it would help in finding out various constraints the state is facing in its development and work out their possible solutions.

Addressing the function as Guest of Honour, Lt. Gen. T.S. Shergill said the Indian army has launched various civic action programmes meant for the welfare of the civilian population of the state. The General sought the cooperation of the people in restoring peace so that in the developmental activities of Manipur, get necessary filip.

Smt. M.K. Binodini Devi, Padmashree while addressing the function wanted awareness campaign on various problems including environmental degradation to be conducted at the grassroot level in localised form instead of holding workshops and seminars at the state or district level. She also expressed her desire to make low cost films to be used as a medium for these campaigns.

In his presidential address, Shri E. Yaima Singh expressed his keen desire to educate the common masses as to why and how the development of the State of Manipur has been hindered. Wishing the Seminar a success, he hoped it would help to find ways and means to remove those constraints, which have been impeding development.

Dr. C.J. Thomas, Deputy Director, ICSSR-NERC, Shillong, introduced the theme of the Seminar and mentioned briefly the activities of the PANACEA and the ICSSR in the northeast India.

Papers presented in all the five academic sessions of the seminar were liked by all those who participated in the deliberations. Some of the papers presented at the seminar were revised subsequently. The responsibility of the views expressed in these articles are entirely of respective authors. Despite of all our best efforts it is possible that mistakes of omission and commission may have crept in this publication. We crave the indulgence of the reader for the same.

C.J. Thomas
R. Gopalakrishnan
R.K. Ranjan Singh

Contents

Part Four
Environment, Population and Industrial Development

Part Five
Women and Language

Contributors

1. Dr. R.K. Ranjit Singh, Reader in Anthropology, D.M. College of Science, Imphal.
2. Mr. Pradip Phanjanbam, Editor, Imphal Free Press, Imphal.
3. Mr. L.I. Singh, Editor, Janata Daily, Imphal.
4. Dr. M.C. Arun Kumar, Department of Anthropology, Manipur University, Imphal.
5. Ms. Ningthonkhongjam Urmila, Lecturer, Department of Political Science, T.S. Paul Manipur Womens' College, Imphal.
6. Mr. Amarjeet Singh, Research Scholar, Department of Sociology, NEHU, Shillong.
7. Professor Ng. Brajachand Singh, Department of Microbiology, HIV Reference Centre and Blood Testing Centre, RIMS, Imphal.
8. Professor Lal Dena, Department of History, Manipur University, Imphal.
9. Dr. B. Manihar Sharma, Life Science Department, Manipur University, Imphal.
10. Professor N. Mohendro Singh, Department of Economics, Manipur University, Imphal.
11. Dr. Priyoranjan Singh, Department of Economics, Manipur University, Imphal.
12. Dr. R.K. Narendra, Demographer, RIMS, Imphal.
13. Mr. N. Sharat, Research Scholar, Department of Anthropology, Manipur University, Imphal.
14. Dr. K.K. Singh Meitei, Manipur University, Imphal.
15. Professor Ksh. Bimola Devi, Department of Political Science, Manipur University, Imphal.
16. Ms. L. Umarani Chanu, Social Worker, working in Loktak Development Authority, Columnist in Poknapham Daily Paper, Secretary Organisation for Women in Need (OWN).

17. Ms. M. Jamuna Devi, Social Worker, working in Continuum Care of AIDS Project, President Development and Empowerment of Volunteers Integration (DEVI).
18. Dr. Gina Shangkham, President, Naga Women's Union, Imphal.
19. Dr. Ch. Yashawanta Singh, Department of Linguistics, Manipur University, Imphal.
20. Dr. Ranjan Singh, Deputy Registrar, Manipur University, Imphal.
21. Professor R. Gopalakrishnan, Department of Geography, NEHU, Shillong.
22. Dr. C. Joshua Thomas, Deputy Director, ICSSR-NERC, Shillong.

Introduction

Manipur reflects a combination of high degree of social fragmentation, stagnating economy and insurgency-dominated activities. Even after five decades of independence, political administrative reforms and planned economic transition, political uncertainty has shown no sign of abatement. In fact, the Manipur is dominated by high population growth, worsening economic relations, rapidly increasing capital, technology and resource requirements, dwindling economic opportunities, fragile law and order situation and so on. Administrators, protagonists and populace have changed and multiplied. Growth of political flora indicated the intensity of fragmentation and fractionalisation of the polity. Access to political power became increasingly sophisticated.

Political uncertainty in such a scale has emerged abruptly. Documentary evidence clearly indicated why the state adopted policies that froze socio-political responses and consolidated hold on these territories. These documents also accounted for the existing ideological constructs and their functions including the pre-1947 insurgency situation. The pre-1947 state brought these areas under its control to further the imperial commercial interests. These areas remained for more backward than any other comparable regions the state. These became colonial possessions protecting mercantile capital. The inhabitants and local power structure frequently asserted themselves only to be crushed, as elsewhere. They succeeded in freezing most of the insurgent activities through military containment.

It was at this point that the note of dissent was voiced in the Manipur. These were in terms of a separate independent political status as voiced by the Naga confederation of people of the questioning of the merger of Manipur with the Indian union. These were not acceded by the state and developed into full scale insurgency. However, with the re-assertion of the state's control, these insurgency situations became protracted and began undermining the socio-economic fabric of the state. Subsequent developments saw gradual spread. So that by late 1990's the state became a region in revolt. Today, when economic liberalisation is gradually transforming the national economy and society, the state is unable to attract the instruments that can telescoped development through massive inflow of capital and technology and in the process substantially transform the material life conditions of the common man. In addition to this, the increasing scale and intensity of natural calamities and immigration have further complicated the scenario.

Escalation of insurgency in the state, then can be attributed to the dynamics of internal geopolitical situation and to negligence and economic stagnation. Regional government remained concerned with strengthening of their electoral base and maintaining status quo, while being unable to effectively implement socio-economic programmes. These fell much short of aspirations of the people and their expectations of socio-economic progress, which led to social fragmentation and polarisation over issues. This encouraged the populace to look upon the protagonists as PANACEA for the socio-economic problems they faced. Subsequent mobilisation achieved cessation of these state run programmes. However, the limited socio-economic transformations and better accessibility conditions increased the level of materialistic hunger of the regional population. This was in direct proportion to the population's inability to satisfy their minimum requirements. In this regard, one can state that the initial decades after 1947 were wasted away in economic development terms. The consequences of which are probably responsible for the libertine decades of the 1970's and 1980's. These compelled the regional administrations to over extend its fragile infrastructural base. This also compelled the rapidly growing working population to become helpless, bewildered, aggressive, and hyperactive; who firmly believed that both the state and the society at large owes them a wages and a place. Yet these beliefs were mediate territorial horizons.

These also titled the equilibrium in the existing structures and opened up the Pandora box. This was essentially in the form of regional administrations effort of pleasing/satisfying the elite pressure groups on the one hand. And on the other hand, meeting the development requirements of the population of the concerned units. However, the protagonists of insurgency movements, by disrupting the regional administration, were able to compel the former to re-identify the priorities and re-allocate the resources. It is obvious then, under these circumstances, economics development went awry.

It is not surprising therefore that both the state and the protagonists of insurgency elicited contradictory responses from the population. Instability parameters normally galvanised the state to address itself to the issues that had brought about it. Instead, half-hearted attempts and protagonists interventions complicated the entire process of development. In a manner of speaking, they followed the principles of Keynesian programmes for re-allocating and re-channelling the priorities and resources to suit the exigencies of the situation. Besides, intervention carries material and moral costs which the population in particular is normally reluctant to bear. This is evident from the situations of status quo, where the population have been manipulated to pay the costs without the possible peace and development in the horizon. Today, all the regional governments and the insurgency groups have countered and check-mated each other. The latter enjoyed definite psychological advantage and were able to compel the population to participate in their programmes aimed at disrupting the state administrative machinery. They were successful in bringing the normal activities of the different political units in the region, to a grinding halt. The moral of the regional administration's personnel reached an all time low. Such instances introduced Domino Effect not only within but also between the administrative units.

Ethnic and political power became the focus of all mobilisation in the state. Economy—its health and the growing need to accelerate its pace, became secondary, although the state of economy was used as a factor in explaining the increasing frequency of conflicts in the state. Various socio-political for a expressed different level of discriminations and deprivation affected due to their subordinate position in the respective administrative units of the region. This, along with the reluctance of the administration encouraged insurgency to spatially expand the levels of operations. Movements against the state intensified, through alliances between the insurgent outfits in the state. This common front in the 1980's, challenged the existing system and its practitioners. These groups also functioned as parallel governments, generating revenue by means that brought instantaneous compliance. This enabled them to increase their level of military preparedness.

At the same time, the regional administration found itself unable to cope up with situations. It was pre-occupied with maintaining the status quo and re-allocated its priorities and resources. They were also notable to effectively counter the psychological pressure exerted by the insurgency movements. They seemed to lose their political will and purpose. Besides, section of the populace and socio-political for a identified themselves with the conflict parameters. This was reinforced when many of these elements infiltrated into administrations. Resources and development came to be unaccounted while available channels were used to strengthen the continued survival of the elite-pressure groups in the region. The population became a mute spectator. It was such a situation that the Federal State intervened to contain the insurgency movement and revive the staggering economy.

It became obvious that with the disruption of the law and order and the stagnation of the economy, the situation in the state had come down to dangerous levels.

However, with the intervention of the federal state, an entirely new ethos emerged. Efforts were directed to restore the political will and purpose as well as increase the morale among the personnel of the regional administration, which was followed by efforts to revive and accelerate the pace of economic development. The attempt to restore normalcy seemed to be ridden with innumerable obstacles and difficulties, the reason being re-alignment of political forces. Thus, at individual or collective levels, it became difficult to categories the political and socio-economic demands and equate the same with the stability. For the various insurgency movements in the state, the return to status quo meant adoption of different tactics. They continued to take advantage to the aberrations in the regional administration and the respective societies while continuing their confrontation at a low key. For the general population, all these developments had profound impact. The state intervention brought with it a uneasy status quo, with perhaps more contenders competing for its limited resources. But, it meant revival of socio-economic programmes and realisation of short term economic initiatives. As an intermediary to restore peace, it was apparent that in order to introduce normalcy inducing conditions, the populace will have to play a more active role.

It is known fact that insurgency has come to stay in the state. Whatever measures that are adopted, it can only restrict level and scale of insurgency and can always resurrect. What can be done is to direct efforts to thwart the rise of any conditions that may encourage such instances. Thus, it becomes obvious that what is needed, is to direct an unimpeded access to developing the economy and induce such conditions to emerge which will direct the necessary resources towards development. The policies need to be based on a force capability framework that induces the development effort. These suggests the necessity of broad policy consensus on the north-east, where continuity in policy is maintained. It should also call for a sound socio-economic policy where changes in administration does not disrupt or alter the economic process. It should involve a mass participation framework. There should be a broad consensus on the individual geopolitical framework for the regional administrative units with appropriate and flexible mechanism. It is at this centre that the workshop entitled constraints in development of Manipur was initiated.

There were nearly 20 participants of which 15 had contributed papers. These fifteen papers have been grouped under five heading of an Introduction (Part 1), Ethnicity, Insurgency, Law and Order (Part 2), Youth, Unemployment, Eradication of Drugs, AIDS (Part 3), Environment, Population and Industrial Development (Part 4), Women and Language as Part 5.

In Part 1 R. Gopalakrishnan provides a working scenario on developments in Manipur. In part 2, R.K. Ranjit Singh, Pradip Phanjanbam and L.I. Singh provides aspects of

In Part 3 M.C. Arun, M. Amarjeet Singh, Ng. Brajachand Singh and Lal Dena, discuss in Student Politics, Problem of Unemployment, Drug Abuse and Role of Church in Conflicts in Manipur.

In Part 4 B. Manithar Sharma, N. Mohendro Singh, Ch. Priyoranjan Singh and R.K. Narendra et al., discuss Impact of Environment, Problem of Industrial Development, Impact of Population Growth in Manipur

In Part 5 Ksh. Bimola Devi, L. Umarani Chanu et al., Gina Shangkham and Ch. Yashawanta Singh deal aspect such as Role of Women in Politics, Manipur Women in Contemporary Situation, Women's Movements in Manipur, Language Development in Manipur.

Conclusion is represented by Recommendation of the Workshop.

Ethnic Movements of the Small Tribes of Manipur: A Preliminary Survey

R.K. Ranjit Singh

This paper aims at explaining the ongoing processes of ethnic movements among the tribes of Manipur. The small tribal groups are invariably involved in some types of ethnic movements in the recent past mainly due to the fact that they are hard-pressed to make social readjustments, undergo socio-cultural transformations and ultimately to adopt various survival strategies.

Multi-ethnic Setting

The geographical location of Manipur has favoured the movements of people from Burma (Myanmar) and India for many centuries. This process, we believe, still continues. Majority of the people of this State belongs to Mongoloid racial stock. Through a process of local miscegenation it has given rise to local populations having distinct physical features. At present the State has 29 Scheduled tribes, 7 Scheduled castes, the Meiteis and the Meitei Pangan (Manipuri Muslim) and representatives of people from different regions of India. A broad picture of the population structure of the State is given in Table 1.

The tibal populations of Manipur are known by the names which are officially recorded in the specific Schedule of the Indian Constitution. Thus the Tangkhul, the Mao, the Hmar, the Purum are some such examples. Officially, Manipur has 29 Scheduled tribes. These tribes range in size from 79 thousand in case of Tangkhul

Table 1. Population of Manipur State in 1991

Category	*Male*	*Female*	*Total*	*P.C.*
Scheduled Tribe	3,22,720	3,09,453	6,32,173	34.5
Scheduled Caste	18,806	18,299	37,105	2.0
Meiteis and other Categories of People—(combined)	5,96,833	5,71,038	11,67,871	63.5
Total	**9,38,358**	**8,98,790**	**18,37,149**	**100**

(1981 census) and as few as 24 individuals in case of Sema. All these tribes align themselves with one or the other of the three ethnic categories in a conventional way as the *Naga*, *Kuki* and *Mizo*. The preliminary attempt on my part to give some kind of ethnic alignment remains incomplete at this level of study. It is because of the fact that the constituent tribes have many other reasons to consider other than the common grounds of cultural, social and linguistic bases in determining their ethnic affiliation. Even within a distinct cultural-linguistic group also there is question of identity difference. Quite aptly one author remarks in the following way: "The tribes of Manipur are often unacceptably classified either into (a) Naga and non-Naga, (b) Naga and Kuki or (c) Naga and Chin-Kuki-Mizo tribes... The generic terms like Naga, Chin, Kuki were given by outsiders for their own easy reference" (Kamkhenthang 1990, 275). It may be pointed out that the tribe of Kuki group mostly subject themselves to a kind of ethnically fluid situation. Such a confusion is brought about by its multiplicity of terms being used to refer to the group. This group is referred to as *Kuki*, *Chin*, and *Mizo*. The same term Kuki was applied to the tribes found in the present Mizoram and the Chin State of Burma. The term was also applied to some tribes of Manipur. Some authors intend to say that the tribes of Manipur other than the Nagas are generally referred to as Kuki. They may be further classified as New Kuki and Old Kuki on the basis of their appearance in Indian side (for example, see J. Shakespear, 1912). In the Chin Hills side of Burma they are known as Chin. Nowadays, as a matter of convention, the Thadou speakers continue to accept Kuki as their name. The same group of people in Burma is designated as Chin while in India they are known as Kuki. The term *Chin* is also exogenous and it means *people of basket* as *Chin* stands for basket in Burmese language. One Paite scholar named Haugo (1971–72) of Mandalay University expressed his displeasure on the application of the term *Chin* to refer to his group. He writes, "It is not only foreign but also derogatory, for it becomes more or less synonymous with being uncivilized, uncultured, backward, even foolish and silly" (cited in Kamkhenthang loc. cit. 277). Paite, Vaiphei, Hmar, the Zou etc. have reached a stage of saturation with the outbreak of tension in Churachandpur area during 1997–98. The type of social relation which existed between these tribes has been described by an author. Many tribes who were supposed outwardly to accept Chin or Kuki disown themselves from these terms. In Manipur the Paite, Hmar and other tribes regard the Thadou speakers as Kuki. In this context, one can state that the Paites are more Chin than any other tribes. By Mizo we mean the Lushai. The non-Lushai speakers are not integrated to the Mizo as the non-Paite speakers in Manipur repulse the term Chin. Chin-Kuki-Mizo group (in the context of Manipur) think that they have nothing to do with Chin. The same attitude is applied to the Thadou speakers in relation to Kuki. In the past several years the Thadou speakers accept to be Thadou Kuki expecting that their cognate tribes also would be a Kuki (Kamkhenthang, loc. cit. 283). In the subsequent years that followed we witnessed a new kind of relationship between the one-time Kuki tribes themselves. This new type of relationship is not conducive to forge unity among themselves as deep-rooted fear psychosis appears to persist between them. As such the problem of "ethnic divides" is not between the traditional lines of the Meitei versus Hillmen or Meitei versus Naga or Meitei versus Kukis. Rather the emergent trend is between the one-time Kuki group of tribes, too.

Thadou-Kuki Controversy

All the Thadou speakers cannot be covered by the term Kuki alone. The tribes which speak Thadou language but who are not Thadou by birth are now unwilling to be Thadou. The explanation for this is that, "Thadou was an eponymous ancestor for only limited clans and he is a junior ancestor to whom the descendants of some ancestors senior to Thadou are unwilling to acknowledge loyalty to Thadou. The fact is that seniority pays more. The tension between Thadou on the one hand and Kuki (a faction of Thadou speakers) run high. For sometime till Thadou dialect along with Paite, Hmar, Tangkhul and Mizo was recognised by the Government of Manipur as medium of instruction in primary stage of education, the speakers of Thadou remain peacefully and blissfully as Thadou or Kuki or Thadou Kuki." (Kamkhenthang *loc. cit.* 283).

Among the Kukis, language factor has a great role to play particularly in forging unity and establishing perpetual social relationships. The Kuki tribes while using their respective dialects or one of the dialects of the tribe, can communicate among themselves. "Thus, the extreme case of language similarity among the Kukis is that of the Thadous and their cognate groups who speak one and the same language popularly known as the Thadou language. Both the groups accepted the term without demur till the dawn of Independence in India as an expression of solidarity. Now, the situation is changed. Instead of accepting it as a common language and as an expression of solidarity, it has unleashed disunity, enmity, tension, conflict and social disharmony among them" (Gangte 1993: 231).

The justification for such a situation is that "The Thadou groups say that the language has been known as 'Thadou language' from time immemorial. It belongs to them, and should therefore, be called 'Thadou language' and nothing else." On the other hand, their cognates claim that the language is not the exclusive possession of the Thadou alone. It is as much theirs, and therefore, should be called 'Kuki language'. At a time when social tension was at the peak, the Government of Manipur issued an order to the effect that Thadou language be read upto Primary stage in school (Government of Manipur, Secretariat: Education Department, Order No. 17/1/72-SE, dated 22-3-1977 cited in Gangte 1993). This was, however, contrasted by the other groups. Conceding the counterclaim of the other groups, the Government of Manipur issued another order (*ibid*: dated 3-1-81 cited in Gangte 1993) which superseded the earlier orders deleting the term 'Thadou' replacing it by "Kuki". The result of such action of the Government had done more harm than good. A Pandora Box had been opened for all concerned (Gangte 1993: 231–32).

The main contention of the 'Thadou' protagonists is that 'Kuki' being the nomenclature denoting other ethnic groups of Kuki who do not speak 'Thadou language' as well, should not be misused, by calling it as 'Kuki language'. The scope and coverage of the nomenclature 'Kuki' must on no account be made narrrow and limited. In the event of the 'Thadou' language' being called 'Kuki language', the term 'Kuki' automatically excludes other ethnic groups of erstwhile 'Kuki' and would, therefore, relegate the nomenclature to the level of group appellations which constitute the term 'Kuki'. The term 'Thadou' which is a personal name must not be treated synonymous to the term 'Kuki' which is a political nomenclature having a far larger meaning and wider scope than the term 'Thadou' (Gangte 1993: 232–33). What is emphasized here is that 'Kuki' is the ethnic name encompassing a number of kindred tribes of which Thadou is but one tribe. Therefore, the term 'Thadou' should not be equated with 'Kuki', which is more embracing term.

Social Implication of 'Thadou'

This issue may be explained slightly in a different way—on the basis of socio-cultural considerations. "The ethnic appellations among the Kukis bear personal names. Thus Thadou is the name of the progenitor of the Kipgen, the Haokip, the Singson (Singsit) and the Sitlhou. Thadou is the younger brother of Doungel and the elder brother of Chongloi, Hangshing and Touthang. The descendants of Thadou being preponderent over the others and also being more famous in reputation colloquially, 'Thadou' has been used to denote all the groups mentioned above collectively. But as time changes, the thinking of the people changes. They have become more conscious of everything names meant for the descendants of Thadou alone, other groups have refused to be so identified since recent past for it carries a deeper social values than superficially taken for granted. Such colloquial usage of the term 'Thadou' has quickened the process of disintegration among the Thadous and their cognate groups. It has, indeed, become the main issue of identity among the Kukis, and has, therefore, become the centrifugal force which drives homogeneous people into divergent tribal groups" (Gangte 1993: 232).

Emergence of Formal Organization

The Thadou is a recognised Scheduled tribe of Manipur whereas Kuki is not. However, Kuki is a recognised tribe of the States of Mizoram, Meghalaya, Tripura and Nagaland. Kuki is taken as a specific tribe of Nagaland. For the furtherance of the cause of the Kuki consolidation a Kuki Tribe Recognition Demand Committee was formed by the speakers of Thadou with an objective of restructuring the list of Scheduled tribes of Manipur. This move has been flatly and vehemently opposed by the Thadou National Council on the ground that the present list of Scheduled tribes of Manipur is good enough as it is done to suit the desire of each tribe by modifying the original order of 1950. In the existing list of tribes there are some tribal clans which have been recognised as independent tribes. "The scheme of putting some clans to the status of tribe is going to be harmful for some tribes like the Paite, Zou and Thadou" (ibid). For instance, the Paite feels it bad when the Guite clans are carved out of the tribal group.

Some important generalizations which we may arrive at after this discussion are:

(i) The speakers of Thadou language but who are not Thadou by themselves cannot accept Thadou or Thadou Kuki to be their tribal names.
(ii) The term (Kuki) cannot bind the different tribes together. It was already disowned by representatives of the tribes (viz., the Paite, Hmar, Zou, Vaiphei, Gangte etc.) leaving Thadou speakers alone to adopt Kuki.

Among other reasons of dissociation of the Thadou from other kindred tribes, a very important factor happened to be Thadous' dominance which the other people do not like. Therefore, these groups of people are on the look out for a suitable term. The term 'Zoumi' or 'Zomi' appears to be more acceptable as it is endogeneous. This term is acceptable to the Zou, Gangte, Hmar, Vaiphei, Paite tribes of Manipur. Literally Zoumi and Mizo have the same meaning. The only difference is that Zoumi is a term used in common parlance and Mizo is a poetic word (Kamkhenthang 1990: 287).

One of the reasons for the emergence of varied opinions among the onetime Kuki groups of tribes is their socio-cultural-ecology in which these tribes are habituated. In the course of their long socio-cultural intercourse with neighbouring tribes, they have imbibed new values and ideas; thus their decision-making processes have been accordingly oriented towards the neighbouring popular groups. Hence we see the emergence of varied opinions which are difficult to be reconciled.

The Thadou and their cognate groups scatter all over Manipur. They also live in pockets of Nagaland and Assam, and they are being influenced by the examples of their Naga neighbours. These groups of the Kukis are the exponents for continuance of the term 'Kuki' as a common identity. The Hmars and the Paites are the second and the third major groups of Kuki, who are found mostly in the southern part of Manipur. They have constant social intercourse with the Chins of the Chin Hills State of Burma and the Mizos of Mizoram. The influence from the Chin Hills State of Burma and from Mizoram have in no small measure contributed to their variegated opinions on the question of common identity. The smaller tribal groups, such as, the Gangte, the Simte, the Vaiphei, the Zou etc. are sandwiched in between the Thadous and their cognates on the one hand and the Hmars and the Paites on the other. The groups are often influenced by the bigger groups on either side of them, and are, therefore, non-adverse to adopting any of the controversial nomenclatures for a common identity, provided such adoption gives all the ethnic groups of the erstwhile Kukis a sense of solidarity and unity (Gangte 1993: 228).

Basis for Ethnic Movements in Manipur

The type of relationships that exists between different groups of people has something to do with the past history of the nation or the state. The historical evidence demonstrates that Manipur has been always provided a broad socio-political framework for integration and frequent assimilation of tribes into the Meitei social formation. In the same way it could be a reason for hatred as well as bitterness between them. The change of identity or the shift of alliance with other groups is not novel development in the context of Manipur. We have examples of groups giving up old identities and accepting new ones. "But there is one significant qualitative difference between the past and the present kind of changing orientation observable among the tribesmen; whereas in the olden times (i.e., in the time of kings) the movement was essentially Meitei-centric, that is to say, small groups redefining their position vis-a-vis the dominant Meitei formation; in the recent (post-independence) times, the tribe realign their identity in what we may term as 'tribe-centric' manner" (Ranjit 1985: 328–29). There is no longer the question of a tribe seeking admission into the Meitei fold nor the Meiteis presently have any political machinery as in the past. It may be mentioned here that, during Kings' time the people who had keen desire of joining the Meitei social system could be formally permitted by the consent of the Meitei king. Since after the official enlistment of Manipur tribes under the Scheduled Tribe List, the change in tribal-level names have become rather difficult. The tribal names so recorded have become more or less a distinct unit of formal as well as official reference. Thus merger of smaller tribes into larger and powerful socio-cultural formation is not very easy, if not possible. Again, the unification drives among the tribe are never towards the larger groups like the Meitei who have different process of social orientation. For instance, the Zemi, Liangmei and Rongmeis prefer to have a larger group by the name of "Zeliangrong". All such movements have reasons to justify their claims. Hence, in the context of Manipur, for that matter the whole of North-East India, the smaller tribes naturally want to join the larger ethnic groups like, 'Naga', 'Kuki' and 'Mizo'. The Naga, Kuki or Mizo represent the highest level of identity, Zeliangrong, for example, represents the intermediate level of identity. The tribal-level identities are the Monsang, Moyon, Koireng etc. which are mostly the reognised official names of these discrete tribes. A number of small tribal groups which still have not yet determined their ethnic affiliation have a tough time to choose one. After determining their choicest reference group all socio-political movements are set into motion. This is the normal process of ethnic movement characteristics of the small tribes of this State.

The Tribes in New Association

Many of the tribes which were classified under 'Old Kuki' by the earlier scholars have now associated themselves with the Nagas. Among them mention may be made of the Anal, Moyon, Monsang, Chothe, Purum etc. Although these tribes have many things in common with the Kuki tribes, it will be unrealistic to say that they are not Nagas in the present context. They have already joined Naga constellation of tribes even before Independence. The historical, geographical, and even the role of leaders and exposure to the modernization process, the roles of media and communication systems all worked together.

The earlier British ethnographers put under the 'Old Kuki' the tribes such as the Anal, Aimol, Purum, Chothe, Lamgang, Kom, Vaiphei, Thikup, Mantak and Ronte, perhaps, on the basis of their linguistc and cultural similarities. The author like J. Shakespear (1912) who is responsible for such a classification, did not make any mention of the tribal names like Moyon and Monsang although these tribes lived side by side with the Anals. These tribes have close cultural as well as linguistic affinities with the Anal as such there is possibility of these tribes being overshadowed by the Anal. Although this type of classification contradicts the present trend of classifying the tribes by the people themselves, the earlier classifications cannot be regarded as baseless.

Many modern scholars will give a classification of tribes of Manipur in the following style: "The tribes of Manipur who are now grouped under the Naga fold are among the earliest inhabitants of the hills of Manipur. The name Naga was given to them by the British administrators with their policy of identifying or classifying the tribes of Nagaland and Manipur. The Naga tribes of Manipur are known by their tribal names. The tribes like Zeme, Liangmei, Rongmei, Mao, Maram, Thangal and Tangkhul and Maring who have strong tradition of common migration with the Northern Nagas of Nagaland on ethnological, linguistic and cultural grounds had been called Naga. There are some tribes like Anal, Moyon, Monsang, Lamgang, Tarao, Chothe, Chiru, Koireng and Kharam who have linguistic affinity with the Kuki-Chin and cultural identification with the Nagas" (Gangmumei 1995: 29).

About the mythical origin of the Nagas a scholar states: "Though the origin and migration of the Nagas as a whole have not been properly settled by the scholars, they pose as one of the challenging identity problems of Naga history... Like some tribes of Nagaland, Manipur's Naga tribes point to Makhel in Mao area as their place of origin, from where they migrated to the present habitat (T.C. Hodson 1911 cited in Gangmumei 1995). There are also traditions among the Naga tribes of Chandel speaking dialects akin to Kuki-Chin, showing their migration from the Chin hills and Kabaw Valley. There is a Tangkhul tradition of migrating from Thaung dut in the Kabaw Valley. The other Naga tribes like Chiru and Koireng who have strong affinity with the Kom and Kharam point to the migration from the southern hills, probably South Manipur and Chin Hills. The Makhel tradition is quite prominent in the history of Naga migration" (Gangmumei 1995: 30).

An important difference which may be brought into focus here is that the tribal names of the past were given by the outsiders on the basis of their cultural or linguistic considerations. In those days village was the unit of all activities and their tribal names was not as important as we have now. The case of "Old Kuki" is a clear example. Mainly because of such reasons many tribes want to disown their earlier names and use new ones which are more acceptable to them. The considerations on cultural or linguistic grounds need not be only rallying factors in determining the names of a tribe. Although the tribes like the Anal, Moyon, Monsang, Purum and the Lamgang were classified with the Old Kukis, they have become Nagas since they deliberately join the latter group of tribes. In such a situation, the ascribed term "Old Kuki" is no longer meaningful or rather it becomes a misnomer. The important factors which induce them in joining the Naga constellation might be their geographical proximity coupled with religious activities and associations thereof. These tribes live close to the Tangkhul and Maring territories. Apart from geographical factor, the decisions of the educated leaders was an important deciding factor in fixing their alliance with other tribes and adopting the common appellation. The roles played by Anal leaders in the pre-Independence political activities of Manipur sets an illustrious example for the generations that follow. The Anals are the people who join hands with leaders of the Naga nationalistic movements in its early stage. Similarly the Moyon and Monsang leaders joined hands in the political activities of the subsequent period. The roles played by the leaders in the political process of the pre-Independence days perhaps determine their future course of socio-political orientations. As mentioned above the new political awareness followed by the heels of their conversion to Christianity. Among these people individual-level conversion to Christianity, particularly among the Anal, Moyon, Monsang, Chothe and Kom goes as far back to the turn of 20th century. Conversion to Christianity among the Moyon, Monsang and Anal was started during 1920s. Thus we notice a close interconnectedness of Christianity with the spread of modern education. The new religion created grounds for regular contacts with different groups of people and establishes ties with them. The regular contacts of the people through religious activities laid the foundation for a perpetual bond between different tribal populations of this region. The earliest ever Christian Missionary activity which started operating in Manipur was the American Baptist Missionary which was spearheaded by Mr. William Pettigrew around 1900.

An important local pastor of this Mission who served among the different tribal areas of Manipur since 1925 was Teba Karong (also called Teba Kom, Teba Kilong or Teba Kom Christian) who received formal education under the care of Mr. William Pettigrew. As a Superintending Pastor he worked in Anal-inhabited areas of southeast Manipur (the present Chandel District) between 1928–1942. In 1947 he took a lead in forming an ethno-political forum by the name of the Khul National Union (for short Khul Union) and of which he was the founder President. The change in his career was directly related to the prevailing political scenario on the eve of India's Independence. A very important development on the part of Manipur tribes was putting together of all the tribes of Manipur into larger political forum to vie for any other political force which may come up. This portion of the history of Manipur is best described by Prim S. Vaiphei in the following paragraphs:

"During 1947–50, the Kuki ethnoses [tribes] with the exception of the Thadous organised themselves in one body and named it Khulmi (means people of the cave) Union [a local corruption of the Khul Union, see above]. The Khulmi was a rival organisation of the Kuki. The Khulmi Union was an organisation of the following tribes: Aimol, Moyon, Monsang, Maring, Mate, Chiru, Chothe, Hmar, Anal, Paite, Gangte, Simte, Kom, Koireng, Lamkang, Vaiphei, Zou etc. Late Mr. Teba Kilong [Teba Karong] and Mr. Tiangkham Paite were the President and the Secretary respectively. The executive body was composed of 1. Dr. Kampu Gangte, 2. Thangkhai Paite, 3. Tawna Hmar, 4. Angnal Anal, 5. Toma [Thoma] Moyon, 6. Ngamdir Moyon, 7. Mono Monsang, 8. Damjakhai Vaiphei, 9. Halpao Mate, 10. Lampum Gangte, 11. Khaikam etc." (Prem S. Vaiphei 1995: 128).

Although the Khul Union emerged as a very popular political organization in the 1948 election of Manipur Legislative Assembly by sending up 7(seven) members viz., Dr. Damjakhai, Dr. Kampu, T.C. Tiankham, Tuljachin, Teba Kilong (Forest Minister), Mono Monsang, Holkhapau Mate members to the Manipur Assembly, the Khul Union did not survive long because of the lack of proper leader (*ibid*).

The proselytization process to which the small tribal populations of Manipur were subjected is now complete. They have invariably become Christians. Thus they no longer move in an inderterminate way. Despite the fact, many of these tribes are in the process of reorienting themselves socially, culturally and even politically towards Naga way of life. Thus they have virtually been moving towards becoming a "part culture" and "part society" of the larger Naga world.

The Koireng Tribe: Still in Search of New Company

For many tribes of this region their ethno-political orientations are already established. However, for some tribes a proper consolidation is yet to be achieved. The Koireng tribe is one such example.

The Koirengs represent a small tribal group of Manipur (949 in 1981) who live mostly in the foot-hills bordering Imphal valley. The tribe is referred to as "Kolhen" (Shakespear 1912), "Quoireng" (Brown 1873, Hodson 1911), "Quoireang" (Mc Culloch 1859) "Kolren" (Grierson 1908), "Kolhan" (Bose 1980–1981). The people themselves believe that the present name of the tribe "Koireng" is the distorted Meitei version of the word "Kolhen", which is probably derived from "Kolren" which means the people of the east (*kol*-east; *hen*-people in Koireng). Viewed from this angle, Grierson's version "Kolren" comes very close to the local usage of the term. As the etymology of the term suggests, the Koirengs are the "people of the east". Due to this fact the people themselves prefer to call themselves "Kolhen" in stead of "Koireng" which according to them is ambiguous. Some sections of the tribe suggest a term "Koren" to mean the title of the divinity of the people of Moirang, a section of the Meitei, used to call "Kolren Lai" which literally means the "God of Koren". The existing official name of the tribe is "Koireng".

A tribe like the Koireng sometimes finds difficulties to survive as an independent socio-cultural entity in the face of steep competitions and struggles which are the order of the day. For their healthy survival as a discrete tribe, they require to articualte themselves with the larger communities to gather political strength or to enlarge their socio-cultural circles. Sometimes the socio-cultural closeness alone may not be the sufficient grounds for forging such an everlasting ethnic partner. The other factors like religion, geographical proximity and the roles of political leaders are important determining factors for their ethnic membership. These are the important strategies which every small tribal group necessarily looks for.

As in the case of the Moyon, Monsang, Anal etc. the Koirengs looked forward for an inter-tribal association. Around 1947 a few tribes like the Kom, Aimol, Chiru, Koireng, Purum and the Kharam formed a socio-cultural association under the name "the Kom Rem Association", after the words *Kom* for the Kom tribe and *Rem* for hillmen. It had a religious wing which started functioning right from 1952. The main activities of the Kom Rem Baptist Churches Association included evangelism and other works for the promotion of Christianity. In 1961 Mr. L. Songkip, the former member of the Sadar Hills Autonomous District Council, was the President of the Kom Rem Association. During his tenur first Kom Rem students' conference was held and by 1962 all the Kom Rem villages of Manipur had joined the Kom Rem Association. As a part of Kom Rem's activities the Koireng people of Utonglok and Sadu Koireng (Senapati District of Manipur) were proselytized. Between 1987–88 the Association had to pass through a rough weather as differences in opinion between the members of the constituent tribes attained its climex. It resulted to a split which gave birth to two associations—the Kom Union and Kom Rem People's Council (K.R.P.C.). The Koireng tribe supported the latter Association (K.R.P.C.). Even after this also a section of the tribes could not tolerate the domineering stance of the Kom tribal leaders. Hence an Association by the name of "Rem" was constituted by the leaders of Koireng, Chiru and Aimol. One educated Chiru leader was the President wereas a Koireng leader worked as Secretary. The Joint Secretary was an Aimol.

During 1990s the tribes like the Koireng and the Chiru received various calls to join the larger groups of tribes. The Hmar people have shown their willingness of accommodating the Koireng within their tribe on the basis of their cultural-linguistic similarities although the attractive forces from the Naga side is equally strong. The educated youths appear to have associational ties with the Nagas in spite of the fact that majority of the general mass want to maintain a neutral position. A proper determination of an ever-lasting alliance with the larger group like the Naga, Kuki, Mizo etc, depends very much on the roles assumed by the educated leaders—the so-called tribal *elites*. They represent the people who have clear vision of the existing problems, having skills to solve difficult problems rationally. Therefore, the general mass rests on the wit of such people who are going to determine their destiny. In case of the Koirengs such *elites* are yet to emerge.

Again the Meitei-centric Identity Movement among the Tribes

In the Senapati District of Manipur, in the midst of prominent Naga tribes like the Mao, Maram and Kacha Naga (Zeme and Liangmei) there is a small tribal group officially called Koirao (919 in 1981). From the earlier evidences we understand that this tribe has been known by different names, such as Kolya, Tangal [Thangal], Khoirao, Meitheipham, Meeyang-khang and officially today as the Koirao. Such a confusion over the tribal name was quite natural because of the fact that tribal-level consciousness was non-existent during those days (in the days of Kings). The important socio-cultural or even political unit was the compact territorial unit in the form of villages. The names like Meeyangkhang [Mayangkhang] or Meitheipham all refer to village settlements inhabited by the Koirao tribe. Even in the Meitei historical records too they were referred to as Thangal to mean the inhabitants of Thangal Surung village of the Koiraos.

The Thangal is one of the Naga tribes. Due to constant contacts with the surrounding populations belonging to Rongmei, Liangmei and Zeme tribes the Thangal tribe has already established regular marital relationships with these tribes. In course of time, due to very regular marital relationships, there has been even the question of changing individual tribal names in favour of these kindred tribes. The people of new generation feel that if this process continues to function any further, the tribe may likely to suffer from many social problems. In apprehension of such a future, the youths of Thangal tribe have joined their hands to counter such attitudes so that the tribal name Thangal be safeguarded.

With the functioning of the Thangal Naga Union (an important formal organisation of the Thangal), the general desire of the people to change their official name "Koirao" in favour of Thangal has been intensified. They claim that Thangal is the original name of the tribe although they are listed as "Koirao" in the Scheduled tribe list of Manipur.

After the close of the British Rule in Manipur, there was a transition of power from the Meitei king to the elected representatives. During this time various tribal groups started forming socio-political groupings, to bring all round development of their society. The Koirao is one of these tribal groups. Such political consciousness appears to have come to the Thangal very late. They became conscious only when the consequence of an age-old practice of marrying wives from outside the tribe (mostly from the Maram tribe) became conspicuous in their local tradition, dialect and customs. It caused anxiety among the Thangal. In view of this they chalked out a plan to put a check on further degeneration of their culture. The Thangal Education Committee was formed in 1947 under the patronage of Mr. Kd. Thaiba of Mapao Thangal village. Primarily the Committee was consituted to propagate and encourage formal education among the Thangals. Later on it became a body which strives to enforce social reformation among the Thangal; it also served as a common platform for all the Thangal people.

On 25th August 1966 the Thangal Education Committee was renamed as Thangal Naga Union. This Union has all the chiefs of Thangal villages as its executive members. To intensify its activities, a youth's wing was formed under the name of the Thangal Naga Students' Union. Right from its inception, besides taking care of the welfare of the people, the Thangal Union has been striving to reaffirm the origin and death of Thangal General and Charai Thangal, another war hero of the Thangal tribe, in the context of the history of Manipur.

The Thangals have a firm belief that Thangal Major, the legendary hero of Manipur (later on called Thangal General) was a Thangal tribe by birth. According to Thangal source, he was born at Thangal Surung village who later on joined the Meitei society during the reign of Gambhir Singh Maharaj (1825–1834). He was affiliated to Kangabam lineage of the Meitei social system and served the king of Manipur in the capacity of a nobleman. An excerpt from a written document of the Thangal Naga Union published in connection with Thangal Day (the 13th August) Celebration of 1980, provides the following accounts: "Thangal General (1817–1891) was born in 1817 at Thangal Surung of Thangal Naga tribe in Sadar Hills, North District [now Senapati district]. He was the eldest son of Shri Saraingamba Thangal of Thangal Surung village. His original name was Lungthoubu...

In 1830, on Tuesday, the 14th August, when Maharaj Pukhramba Tangkhomba [?] came to catch elephant near Ekou, "Thangal General" [then] (Lungthoubu) was guiding the party and they cought one she elephant with a calf. The bravery and strength of Thangal General was greatly admired by the Maharaja who wanted to take him to Sana palace for the service of the people of Manipur. Accordingly Lungthoubu's service was utilized in Sana palace by the Maharaja at the age of 14. He served Manipur from the reign of Shri Gambhir Singh upto the reign of Shri Kulachandra Singh" (op. cit. 9). Apart from this account given by the Thangals we get plenty of material furnished by different authors. Each author gives accounts which do not maintain any uniformity. For the purpose of illustration we may take the instance of Sir James Johnstone's account on Thangal General. He writes, "Thangal Major was a remarkable character, and had a chequered history. Thangal Major was one of the props of the throne when Gambhir Singh ascended it. He had been introduced at the court at an early age, and accompanied the Rajah in an expedition against the village of Thangal inhabited by the tribe of Naga. He was given the name Thangal in memory of the event" (Johnstone 1971: 75). No doubt, Thangal Major was a very prominent figure in the history of Manipur. We have sufficient accounts on his activities; however, no clear identity, to conform to those of the Thangals' claim is available so far. A Meitei scholar's view on Thangal's identity is very much in the normal way of identifying a Meitei individual. His view is based on the statement given during the trial in connection with the killing of British officials. The statement was made in the court of the Chief Political Officer, Manipur on the 25th May 1891, a few months before his death by hanging in the public on the 13th August 1891. Thangal General said that he was the son of Khetri Singh Manipuri of village Angom Leikai, aged 85 years. He was a Piba (eldest male issue of the eldest surviving line of a family) of Chingamakha Taba Kangabam family of Ningthouja Salai of the Meiteis. He was a descendant of Meidingu Yaraba who ruled in Manipur (799–821 A.D.) and was the 18th line of descendent from Meidingu Yaraba (Khelchandra 1997: 1–2).

The Thangal Naga Union's objective at the moment is to get the valour and fame earned at the cost of Thangal General's life for the cause of the people of Manipur be perpetuated in the name of the tribe by retaining the tribal name "Thangal". The movement on the part of Thangal tribe is already launched as early as 1980. Whether they get their aspirations fulfilled or not, the tribes have explored a new platform where formal discourse over the relationship of the Thangal tribe with the Meitei may be regularly held. Some day we may be able to solve the riddle through proper empirical studies. The main activities lying in front of the Thangal Naga Union include the protection of their identity and to accelerate developmental process. The other issues other than those are as follows:

i. To rectify the term 'Koirao' and change it to their original name 'Thangal' in the Scheduled Tribe list of Manipur.
ii. To introduce the Thangal dialect in the All India Radio tribal programme.
iii. To construct memorial hall—one for Thangal General at Thangal Surung and another for Charai Thangal at Mayangkhang village (Source: Latif Shah and Ranjit Singh, 1999).

The Manipur situation clearly indicates that the various tribes of this region had already got different experiences in the course of history. In the historical period they happened to be allies, foes, or even the subjects of the Meitei kings. Despite this fact, the post-independence picture is quite different. The strong force emanating from different powerful nations of this region have already waned. Consequently they have been left to choose their own destiny. During this period, the roles of the educated political or religious leaders were quite important. Whatever course they fix for the tribe or community to follow has now emerged as the guiding force to the succeeding generations. Consequently, the Moyon, Monsang as well as the Anals have already got a determined direction for their socio-political orientations and goals. And as such movements are already set into motions. Therefore, almost all the tribal ethnic movements whatever we may come across in the present-day Manipur can be analyzed and understood from these perspectives. As indicated above, the linguistic, cultural or even religious factors alone may not be the right pointers of ethnic movements of the small tribes of this region.

REFERENCES

Bose, J.K. 1980. *Glimpses of Tribal Life in North East India*. Institute of Social Research and Applied Anthropology, Calcutta.

Brown, R. 1873. *Statistical Account of the Native State of Manipur*. Office of the superintendent of Govt. Printing, Calcutta.

Gangte, T.S. 1993. *The Kukis of Manipur: A Historical Analysis*. New Delhi, Gyan Publishing House.

Grierson, G.A. 1908. *Linguistic Survey of India* (Reprint 1967) Vol. III Delhi: Motilal Banarsidass.

Hatchinson, R.H.S. 1978. *Chittagong Hill Tracts* (Reprint) Delhi: Vivek Pub. Co.

Hodson, T.C. 1911. *Naga Tribes of Manipur* (Reprint 1987) Low Price Publication, G.O.I Press, Calcutta.

Iboongohal Singh, L. and N. Khelchandra Singh 1967. *Cheitharol Kumbaba* Manipur Sahitya Parishad, Imphal.

Johnstone, S.J. 1971. *Manipur and Naga Hills,* Vivek Publishing House, Delhi.

Kabui, Gangmumei 1987. *The Koirengs of Manipur,* Koren Historical Research Committee, Imphal.

Kabui, Gangmumei 1995. Genesis of the ethnoses of Manipur in *Manipur Past and Present*, Vol. III, N. Sanajaoba (ed). Mittal Publications, New Delhi.

Kamkhenthang, H. 1990. Identity crisis among the Tribes of Manipur *Nationality, Ethnicity and Cultural Identity*, B. Pakem (ed). (275–289). Guwahati, Omson Publications.

Khelchandra Singh, N. 1997. *Thangal General*, Thangal General Sagal Committee, Imphal.

Mc Culloch 1859. *Accounts of the Valley of Manipur*, Calcutta.

Prim, S. Vaiphei 1995. The Kukis in Manipur in *Manipur Past and Present* Vol. III, N. Sanajaoba (ed.). Delhi: Mittal Publication.

Ranjit Singh, R.K. 1985. *The Monsang Tribe of Manipur: A study in Changing Social Orientation of Small Tribal Group*. Ph.D. thesis (unpublished), Dibrugarh University, Assam.

Ranjit Singh, R.K. 1988. Emergent Ethnic Processes in Manipur in *Manipur Past and Present*, Vol. I. N. Sanajaoba (ed.). Mittal Publications, Delhi.

Shah, Latif and R.K. and Ranjit Singh 1999. *The Koirao (Thangal) Tribe of Manipur* T.D.B.C. Govt. of Manipur.

Shakespear, J. 1912. *The Lushai Kuki Clans* Delhi: Central Publishing House (Reprint 1985).

Thangal Naga Union. 1980. *The Thangal Day*.

Insurgency and its Impact on the Development of Manipur

Pradip Phanjanbam

Inhibition of the growth of industries in the northeast as a result of insurgency can be broadly classified under two heads. One is direct, the other indirect. In the first category, investment is shied away by the sense of fear that insurgents may interfere directly through extortion, intimidation or else the industry in which the investment is being made may get caught in unintentional but all the same dangerous crossfire, just as the Japan sponsored sericulture project was. It may be recalled how in the month of June, a Japanese engineers team detailed to do the ground work for this project got themselves into a dangerous situation when members of a particular insurgent group sought shelter in the rented accommodation they were putting up. In an encounter that resulted in the house, six militants were killed. Luckily the Japanese team was out of the house when the encounter took place, saving a lot of diplomatic complications.

The second manner in which industrial growth is inhibited in an insurgency situation is indirect, or should we say less direct. It has to do with counter insurgency. The establishment in its effort to contain insurgency, has not time to think of meaningful investment elsewhere, other than in acquiring counter insurgency implements. Hence the government's preference in these states has been more towards buying guns and ammunition, raising counter insurgency forces, etc. rather than buying tractors, fertilisers and other investments which can augment the availability of bread and butter.

This is the immediate situation. A trap from which it is difficult to escape. Each of the two scenario has its own logic. The insurgents are fired by revolutionary ideals and zeal. The war at hand for them is above all. In fact in their vision of things, industries and growth are inhibited precise because at a certain stage, political and historical progress have become wrapped by extraneous circumstances. Correcting these and setting them on the track they believe is the right course is the top priority for once this is done, all else will fall in place. Industries, development, growth all will follow naturally, is their belief. That others think this is not much more than a Utopian dream is another matter all together. But even those opposed to insurgency are by the forces of circumstance blinded to other vital calls of the society. As much as the insurgents are blind to the needs of the hour, so are those involved in counter insurgency. It is such an overwhelming problem which leaves little time or energy with anybody caught in it to think or see much beyond the immediate. This is true of even the Press. If insurgency is not news, nothing else is. Those who have been reading the local newspapers will agree. From the ordinary man on the streets, to the top planners in the corridors of power, thoughts of insurgency cannot ever be far from the mind. It has eaten into the beings of the place as well as everybody in it. Obsession is the word to describe it. How else can it be?

Who is responsible for this situation? How has this come about? Where are the roots of these problems? These are no easy questions, but the search for an answer cannot be given up. For only then can the trap disappear. As they say insurgency is a state of the mind. It cannot be destroyed physically, which explains why it has remained despite the most ferocious of counter insurgency measures. In fact such measures only harden the state of mind. It also mutates the mindset of the society making it more destructive, unreasonable and dangerous.

One of the most familiar refrains in all homilies on the reasons for the economic backwardness of Manipur and so also other northeastern states is that it is the phenomenon of militancy that is keeping the inflow of capital into the area, thus keeping all developmental activities arrested. There is no doubt much truth in this. Militancy has kept away capital investments in the state. The manner in which even such a welcome and high profile undertaking as the Japan sponsored sericulture project tottered because of the fallouts of militancy is a case in point. We can quite imagine the number of other potential areas of industrial and other forms of development related investments, particularly from the private sectors, domestic as well as foreign, that have been shied away by the fear of the law and order situation in the state. So when other more advanced states are talking of building information highways by tying up with big names like Micrcsoft and Dell, our own state is unable to even repair and maintain its miserable network of surface roads, virtually cutting off large sections of its population for prolonged periods during every monsoon when the rains either cause landslips or else render the un-metalled roads un-motorable.

But the argument of militancy as a development inhibitor has a counter argument. As believers in development as a process that must begin from below, catalysed by assistance and blessings from above, we find this angle of vision very interesting. If militancy has resulted in non-development, it is equally true that non-development has led to militancy to a great extent. It is worthwhile noting that even before militancy broke out, there has been virtually no development in these regions. As a matter of fact, there has been a quantum jump in the size of the state budgets as well as other Central largesse ever since militancy raised its head, giving credence to the argument that it was militancy that made the planners sitting above notice the plights of these state. Once the chicken and egg situation has been set into motion, it is a never ending cycle in which each negatively reinforce the other, until both grow into monstrosities. In this way, we are of the opinion that the fearsome turbulence witnessed in the region today is a price our societies are paying for years of insensitivity and abuses. If the establishment is harangued today, it is because it has for far too long taken the avenging power of the social mechanism as well as its history, for granted. The saddest part of the story is, we still have not learnt the lesson. We continue to refuse to acknowledge that the society is very much like a living organism, which is able to, or else vulnerable to, like all living things, fall sick, led astray, be hungry or angry. We continue to ignore the malevolence with which trapped energy within the society can be unleashed. Every corrupt act, every fair competition stifled, every man cheated, every wrong done, every hope crushed by bribery and nepotism, all add to this residue of violent and destructive energy within the social organism. Individually, each bit of this energy may seem insignificant, but these can be accumulated to certain critical points and then explode. The explosion that we are witnessing today, hence we like to contend, can be treated as mutated society hitting back at us—its abusers.

Unrest among ethnic minorities, tribals and indigenous peoples, is not an isolated occurrence in India alone. It is a problem that has stricken the entire post-colonial world. In their urgency to find and assert their national identities, the former colonies, upon their release from the yoke of colonialism, have not been able to, or bothered to give much attention to the needs and aspirations of smaller nationalities within their own geographical boundaries. Very often again, the unfeeling attitudes of the dominant and overriding nationalisms and the policy programs dictated by them have resulted in the destruction of the existence of minority ethnic communities of indigenous peoples as viable groups, a phenomenon that has been described as ethnocide. Two principal beliefs of most recently decolonised nations are responsible for ethnocide within them. One is the zeal to obliterate all pre-modern forms of economic organisations in the name of ushering in a progressive modern economy and the other is the equally fervent belief that all sub-national ethnic units must necessarily surrender themselves totally and merge into the larger nation-state, a phenomenon often sublimated as joining the mainstream of national life, in the name of national unity. Such policies, as history is witnessing today in many parts of the world, including in India's northeastern region, have given rise to more problems than they have solved.

The world community has today, by and large recognized the need to spare attention to this vexing problem. The United Nations has itself become a forum for the redressal of problems faced by the various ethnic groups all over the world. In fact, in view of the resurgence of ethnic and indigenous peoples, the UN declared the decade beginning 1995 as the UN decade of the indigenous people. Since the early 1990s, at least three underground groups from India's northeast region, namely the National Socialist Council of Nagaland, NSCN (Isak-Muivah), followed by the United National Liberation Front, UNLF, of Manipur, and the United Liberation Front of Assam, ULFA, have been allowed to give their representations before the international body almost annually at the meets that it organises on the issue of the problems faced by the world indigenous peoples. Other than this, the NSCN (I-M) has also been admitted into the Unrepresented Nations and Peoples' Organisation, UNPO, a newly formed pressure group based in The Hague.

In many ways, the upheavals of the ethnic indigenous communities in the northeast regions borders the tragic. It is the story of different tribal groups and communities, long isolated from the outside world, rudely awakening to a different reality in which they stand the danger of being drowned or at best occupying a subordinate position. Theirs is a struggle to come to terms with it. The most aggressive of these struggles have chosen to totally reject the destiny they have been thrown into and look for it elsewhere, away from the general trend of history. A no mean task, and as we have seen, very often leads up blind alleys. For the ethnic minorities, it is one of the cruel junctures of history they have found themselves in. The choices before them are either a total surrender to a fate in which their identities as viable groups are endangered or else swim against the intimidating and incessant tides of the historical mainstream.

This threat to the group identity of the ethnic communities may not have been wilfully induced by the mother countries. On the other hand, they may be making efforts in the best way they understand the situation to prevent such a thing from happening. It is rather a situational tragedy. The ethnic groups spiritually or mentally do not belong to the new environment they are exposed to, hence are unable to easily adjust or find a firm footing in it. The result is a sense of deprivation and dislocation. Most often they end up withdrawing within themselves as an intuitive resistance to the forces of change or else end up as spiritual wrecks in their effort to assimilate into the new system. Individuals have succeeded in finding their places in the new environment, but as groups, the experiment is still on, and the signs so far have not been very encouraging.

The animosity of the ethnic communities in the northeastern states reserved for the non-tribal traders from the plains of mainland India is a case in point. In Manipur, the locals know them as "Mayang", in Mizoram "Vai", in Meghalaya "Dakhar" and in Nagaland just "Indian". In the eyes of the locals, among others, they represent the agents of change that have intruded into their lives to dislocate and dismantle their old world. In the beginning they were welcomed guests, as they brought in new comforts from the outside world. However, not long after, when they started controlling the entire economy of these places, they came to be despised as usurpers. Catalysing this change of attitude is the fact that the traders from outside, as a class, never tried to be captains of industries in the region. They much preferred to remain as traders with the primary motive of profiteering as their inspiration. In the social and cultural spheres too they remained aloof from the local population hence generations after their arrival in the region, they remained somewhat as aliens. Because of this, their control of the economy of the place came to be viewed as a kind of colonisation. Wresting the control from the outsider traders by competition by the locals was out of question. Whereas the outsider traders had trading in their blood for centuries, the locals had come in contact with the new "monetary economy" barely a generation or two ago. Moreover, the locals were accustomed to the leisurely pace of the pre-modern economy and their laid-back approach robbed them of the competitive edge in the fast and hectic new environment they found themselves in. This failure often led to frustrations and envy, mixed with an acute sense of being usurped. On the job front too, it was once again a fresh wave of well trained professional non-locals who have had the benefits of Western education long before the first primary school was opened in the region, who cornered the choicest slices. The transfer of the economic reins from the hands of the locals to those of the outsiders was thus complete. Forced into the back seat, the ethnic communities start looking inwards for salvation rather than to the new forces of change.

Culturally too, the ethnic communities find themselves gradually marginalised. Constantly and incessantly bombarded with well packaged, often illusory pictures of affluence and wellbeing from the dominant cultures through the much advanced mass media particularly the television, the ethnic communities who were already disoriented in the new world, begin to feel themselves as inferiors. This psychology further worsened their chances of adopting and coming to terms with their changed situation. Because the communication flow is virtually one-way, that is, from the dominant to the weaker cultures, the burden of the adverse fallouts of this cross-cultural communication is felt only by the weaker cultures. Multiplying this effect is the breakneck pace with which the mass media technology has been advancing in the modern times. Even relatively more advanced societies have been outstripped in this race with technology. Invariably backward regions like the northeast states have also been rather peculiar. Development has never been organic in that it has not grown out of the internal pressures built from the collective needs of the region at any given point of time. Rather than this, development has been delivered in packages as part of the statutory largesse distributed by the Central Government from time to time.

As for instance, when television first came to the northeast in 1982, it was straight away colour television. The black-and-white hinter period, and the long, impatient wait for the colour television were altogether skipped. Before the people ever had time to absorb and internalise the entry of this medium into their lives, cable-television arrived, followed in quick succession by satellite television. The gestation period for adjustment to the new environment created by the introduction of each of the advancement in technology was barely available. Growth in technology has never been systematic or regulated for the social organism of the ethnic groups to digest and absorb to their best benefits.

The youth, particularly the urban and semi-urban, idle, lumpenised category, whose numbers are on a rapid increase, are the worst hit. The images of comfort and other trappings of the modern consumerist cultures, which are basically meant for the consumption of affluent societies, also flood their minds. The result is the creation of illusory and often detrimental ideals in their minds. Illusory, because their objective economic realities are not commensurate with the ideals set for them by these images. Hence, the result is a wide disparity between what is achievable by them and what they had been made to believe is within their reach. Between their individual expectations and their society's capacity to afford these expectations. The resultant sense of being let down often leads them to socially deviant behaviours such as drugs abuse, alcoholism, promiscuity, juvenile delinquency etc. among the youth of the ethnic groups.

For the affluent societies, these images are nothing unnatural to their lifestyles and hence are less likely to create any discordance. Moreover, the youth of the affluent societies have adequate protections against the harmful effects of the consumerist ideals as a result of education, high standards of living, and above all a social ethos that is able to put these ideals in the correct perspectives. In this way they are less vulnerable than their ethnic counterparts in the backward regions of the country.

Slowly but surely, the ethnic cultures begin withering away. Because the objective conditions are not ripe, the new values that have come in are not able to fill the vacuum left by the disappearance of the traditional. The end result is the emergence of a rootless, lost generation. A generation that ends up as bad imitations at best, if not caricatures of the affluent, dominant societies. The aimless drift of a derelict generation of zombies and lotus eaters begins. Rather than inherit the spirit and the vibrancy of the societies they try to emulate, they end up being stricken with the worst of their scourges. Acquired Immuno Deficiency Syndrome, AIDS, is just one of these. It is not a coincidence that some of the northeast states, like Manipur, rank as some of the most prone areas to drugs and AIDS in the whole of India.

Total failure of understanding of the moral dilemma of the ethnic communities, rather than dearth of goodwill, has also hastened this decay process. Liberal doses of fund have been poured into these states year after year amidst the social milieu of rot and decay. In the absence of any tangible plan or accountability, the liberal funds prove to be as harmful to the moral health of the ethnic societies as much as medicinal drugs administered in overdoses become poisonous to the patient. Easy money is addictive, just as much as narcotic drugs and it has devastated the work culture of these societies. Here, money is no longer measured in terms of sweat, hence its real worth is no more known. A parasitic economy that is far from self-generating but rather solely dependent on the charity of the Central Government has today evolved in most of these states.

A coterie also emerges. While the overwhelming masses remain untouched by the liberal benefits of the establishment, this coterie and their children grab the best of them including the funds. Wealth is no more the fruit of labour or enterprise, but becomes the result of organised and protected robbery. Consequently, rich people are no longer respectable people. This crop of newly sown middle-class coterie are bereft of the dynamism or the spirit of creativity that the bourgeoisie elsewhere, however self-centred on reactionary, is known for. Greed, avarice and selfishness become their hallmark. They dominate the government, that is, the state politics and bureaucracy, and succeed in reducing it to a big force. They bring in rampant and shameless corruption in the administration and make political horse-trading, in which political loyalties are bought and sold for a price, into a fine art. Rather than provide the leadership to guide the destinies of their societies at its times of crisis, they further hasten the process of decay by destroying completely the people's faith in the state machinery.

Resistance against this process of decay was expected. When it does arrive, it takes the extreme form. First the revivalist groups who looked for inspiration from the past glories of their societies entered the scene. They were followed by the revisionists who thought it was possible to redo certain portions of history that was offending to their sensibilities. The reformists were next in line. Then before anybody realised it, the mutant offspring of the much abused societies appear on their social firmament. These epitome of the blind, directionless fury that had been building up within these societies for years are impatient to listen to the rationalisation of the decay process. They set about blasting away anything they thought was the cause of this decay. The days of the militants have arrived.

In the words of Jean Paul Sartre, if this fury fails to find an outlet, it turns in a vacuum and devastates the oppressed creatures themselves. In order to free themselves they even massacre each other. The different tribes fight between themselves since they cannot face the real enemy—and you can count on colonial policy to keep up their rivalries; the man who raises a knife against his brother thinks that he has destroyed once and for all the detested image of their common degradation, even though these expiatory victims don't quench their thirst for blood.

Likewise, factional fights, ethnic war, communal flare-ups have become commonplace in the northeast region. The tension and friction all around is palpable and eerliy dangerous.

Very soon, this blind rage finds direction. The art of politics is simply transformed into the art of war; the political militant is the rebel. To fight the war and to take part in politics; the two things become one and the same thing. The revolution is born.

This explains why the different underground organisations enjoy wide sympathy among the people they operate. For these people, whose morales are at their lowest ebbs, the militant groups symbolise in many ways, the resurgence of their lost pride and manhood—a reassurance that there is still fight left in their depleted souls. The militants become their method and vehicle for delivering their own anger at the system that was corroding away their beings, Rapidly weakening and helpless populations on the desperate lookout for a prop to lean against, find just that in the "revolutionary" parties that have sprung up amidst them.

The moot question is, are all this leading to a dead end? Will the northeast agenda even be completed wholly? Can lasting peace ever return to the northeast? Yes, but only if the ethnic communities of the region have been given their rightful and respectful places in the nation of nations. Yes, but only if the "mainstream" expands to accommodate the "sub-streams" without their having to surrender their distinctive characteristics, by having to merge totally into it. Only by inculcating such a confidence among the insecure peoples of the northeast can there be hope for a final solution to the never ending, undeclared war in the region. The agenda is clearly open before the nation.

In recent times, there have been some welcome signs of a political will to tackle the problems of the northeast in earnest. The initiative was made towards the end of 1996 by the then Prime Minister of India, H.D. Deve Gowda, who made a whirlwind tour of the region at the time and announced a Rs. 6000 crore "northeast economic package" at the end of it. It is worth noting that no Prime Minister had visited many of the states for a long time when he suddenly decided to show up. As for instance, it was more than eight years after Rajiv Gandhi as Prime Minister visited Manipur that the state received Gowda. It is true that the "northeast package" has still not been opened as yet, but more that the money, it is a different vision of the northeast than he had ushered in amongst the Central leaders. He did not remain in office for long, but the Prime Minister who succeeded him, Inder Kumar Gujral, too followed the tract he cut. One of his first tour destinations was the northeast. He also decided continue with Gowda's northeast policy. Gujral too did not stay for long. Now, a new Prime Minister, from a new political party, Atal Behari Vajpayee, of the Bharatiya Janata Party, BJP, has announced his northeast policy, picking up the issue where Gowda and Gujral left it. The new-found attention on the northeast has come as a whiff of fresh air to the suffocating atmosphere that had been prevalent in the region for a long time. The spirit is one of openness. If not anything else, what it has done is to shower hope on those concerned by the problem. However, it is only the beginning—a good beginning at that. Anything and everything can still go wrong. But if nothing goes wrong, and if the intentions remain honourable and steadfast, there is a hope that some light may become visible at the end of the dark tunnel.

Problems of Law and Order in Manipur

L.I. Singh

Peace and Prosperity

Endeavouring to gain and to maintain peace and harmony, prosperity and social justice is the objective and vow of any Government of any state. But venture for the Chief of Ruler and the struggle for survival are act of ignoring the movement for peace and harmony, prosperity and social justice. Keeping act of venture and struggle is required in check and balance instead of nullification. Because, "Life is struggle, hence no struggle no life". It is a very rational one.

Struggle for Freedom of India was not merely a struggle for political freedom from foreign rule but also a struggle against social evils and feudalism. It gave awareness of human duties and rights.

Netaji Subhas Chandra Bose said," Freedom implied not only emancipation from political bondage but also equal distribution of wealth, abolition of caste. barriers and social inequities and destruction of communalism and religious intolerence." This quotation was the weapon for Freedom Struggle and an idea for the Constitutional making body of Indian Republic. We can see the idea as the source of the Preamble of our Constitution that is "*We the People of India,* having solemnly resolved to constitute India into a *Sovereign Socialist Secular Democratic Republic*". We know a Democratic Republic is the best guarantor of Human Rights. Our people are liberated by our Constitution from all oppressive measures and provides us good laws for the protection of our individual liberty.

But, act of terrorism does not question Human Rights and Civic Sense. Prime Minister Shri Atal Behari Vajpayee said," Terrorism is the ultimate denial of Human Rights. Nations faced with the spectre of terrorism find themselves in a difficult situation. They are weighed down by the responsibility towards the protection of Human Rights as well as violation of Human Rights by terrorists."

Such a phenomenon is very concerned all over the country particularly in the North-Eastern States and Jammu and Kashmir.

Manipur State

Manipur is a geographical expression. It has been in existence from time immemorial. It lies between latitude 23.80 degree and 25.68 degree North and longitude 93.03 degree and 94.78 degree East and is bounded on the north by the Naga Hills (now Nagaland), on the East by Burma (now Myanmar), on the South by the Chin Hills (Myanmar) and Lusai Hills (now Mizoram) and West Cachar District (Assam). Its boundary and topography is the Gift of Nature. The state has different tribes and castes having distinct genology as well as different dialects and culture. Manipuri language (Meiteilon) is the inter-communicating language. No authority in the world has the right to propose for changing the Manipur Map. Existing Manipur Map is a self-evident truth (an axiom).

After a prolong struggle, Manipur was upgraded from the status of Union Territory (Original Part—C State), by the North Eastern Areas (Reorganisation) Act, 1971 and full-fledged statehood was granted to Manipur on 21st January, 1972 which was inaugurated by the then Prime Minister, Smt. Indira Gandhi.

Present Government

Now, we have our own 7th Law Making Body (Legislative Assembly) and Council of Ministers comprising 33 members led by Shri Wahengbam Nipamacha Singh as Chief Minister. His Government, the United Front Government which comprises of Manipur State Congress Party, Federal Party of Manipur and Independents, claimed of bringing peace, communal harmony and prosperity, commendable success in the counter-insurgency front, and the Government had constituted a body known as Manipur Human Rights Commission on June 27, 1998. This claim is only a face-saving act of this Government.

Law and Order Situation

Actually, the present law and order situation has been adversely affected by the violent and subversive activities of the various extremist groups and outfits operating in the state since more than the last two decades, and continuing in the state till as yet.

The ethnic clashes in the Hills also create a feeling of insecurity and mutual distrust. The ethnic clashes are still unable to be totally subsided, it occurs any time at any where. By the above facts and circumstances, unavoidably, the state continues to be declared as a Disturbed Area under the Armed Forces Special Powers Act.

Peace Process of Ethnic Clash of Churachandpur

Peace initiative was started by the Chief Minister Shri Rishang Keishing (now a sitting MLA) himself, who, on his first visit to Churachandpur District on 26-6-1997, formed the Peace Committee comprising of responsible leaders of various tribes including Kukis and Zomis who have close affinity with the Mizos. Shri Rishang Keishing, Chief Minister of the state, requested Shri Lalthanhawla, Chief Minister of Mizoram, for support and co-operation who instantly sent a 'Goodwill Team' led by Shri Chawnkunga, Agriculture Minister of Mizoram. On the initiative of Dr. Chalton Lien Amo, the then Minister of State (Medical) of Manipur, the KNF and ZRA agreed "to seize all offensive activities" including killing, kidnapping, burning down of houses, wanton destruction of any kind, etc. for a period of 30 days, w.e.f. 11-8-1997. Besides, a Peace Rally was organised on the initiative of Meitei Society of Churachandpur and All Manipur Students' Union and other Voluntary Organisations in which about ten thousand people belonging to various communities participated.

After that, Shri Wahengbam Nipamacha Singh, the present Chief Minister visited the District. He felt the necessity of forming a state level committee so as to enable the state Government to garner all the resources at its command to bring about a permanent peace in the district. Accordingly, a state level Peace Committee, with the Chief Minister as Chairman, was constituted. To facilitate the functioning of the Committee, a Sub-Committee, under the Chairmanship of the Deputy Chief Minister, was also constituted on 10-3-1998. The first Sub-Committee meeting, held on 22-3-1998, unanimously resolved to work for peace in Churachandpur District and all forms of violence, offensive and counter-offensive activities be shunned with immediate effect.

As a result, a Memorandum of Understanding (MOU) was finally reached and signed on 26-3-1998 at Churachandpur after a marathon meeting. The Memorandum of Understanding was valid for 28 days during which it was agreed to stop all forms of violence including even use of harsh words and sort out the differences so as to enable to sign a permanent peace agreement.

As a follow-up of the MOU, a Monitoring Cell with Shri Hangkhanlian, Hon'ble Minister as Chairman was constituted. To assist the Monitoring Cell, a Sub-Committee to Monitoring Cell was also constituted on 26-3-1998. Since the signing of the MOU, peace gradually returned to Churachandpur and no untoward incident reported although some tension prevails which can be attributed to the long running ethnic strife.

As the MOU was a temporary arrangement, the need for a permanent peace accord continues. Therefore, a meeting was held on 16-4-1998 with the Chief Minister in the Chair at the Mini Secretariat of Churachandpur District Headquarters and it was agreed to extend the MOU by another 30 days i.e. upto 26-5-1998. Again, a High Level Committee meeting was held on 15-5-1998 and extended the time for another 30 days i.e. upto 30-9-1998.

Finally, as a token of customary apology for mowing down ten innocent lives and injuring another four persons in the night of 24th June, 1997 at Saikhul village by the KNF thereby dragging the two communities in conflict, the Kuki Inpi offered a feast by killing a four legged animal, a bull (Bawngtal) on the 29th September, 1998. In a very cordial atmosphere and mutual trust, the feast was happily shared together by leaders of the Kuki Inpi and the Zomi Council. In response to the good gesture shown by the Kuki Inpi, the Zomi Council showed their goodness and love for peace in the form of killing another four legged animal, a pig (Voktal), the following day the 30th September, 1998 which was also happily shared together by both communities' leaders.

Agreement

Both the parties agreed upon the following points:

* That, the nomenclatures Kuki and Zomi shall be mutually respected by all Zomis and Kukis. Every individual or group of

persons shall be at liberty to call himself or themselves by any name, and the nomenclature Kuki and Zomi shall not in any way be imposed upon any person or group against his/their will at any point of time.

* That, any person who has occupied or has physical possession of any land/private building/houses and quarters wrongfully and illegally during the period of clashes shall return and restore to the rightful owner, such lands and buildings.
* That, no Kuki or Zomi Military shall indulge themselves in any forcible collection of funds, taxes etc. against their counterpart nomenclature, be it from the Government Officials, individuals, contractors and business establishments.
* That, all points of MOU's between the Kuki Inpi and the Zomi Council shall be operative and binding to all concerned persons and parties including the Government.

Signed this 1st October, 1998 on behalf of Kukis and Zomis respectively.

Sd/-	Sd/-
(Albert Gen. Gauknup Mate)	(K. Vungzalian)
President	Chairman
Kuki Inpi, Churachandpur	Zomi Council
Dt. 1/10/1998	Dt. 1/10/1998

Such practice of peace process is law of Machiavellianism.

Situation of the State

The state of Manipur has been facing serious problems of the valley based and hill based insurgent groups and law and order.

As per record, the acute shortage of manpower, weapons, vehicles etc. the State Police Department with the aid of the CRPF, Assam Rifles and Army achieved a commendable success in the counter insurgency front. During the period from 1-1-1999 to 31-12-1999, altogether 1070 extremists belonging to various underground outfits were arrested and 49 others killed by the police/ Security Force while a total of 220 numbers of assorted weapons like L.M.G., M-16, AK-47/56 Rifles, U.M.G. etc. were recovered from the extremists by the police/Security Force along with 5,186 rounds of ammunition. Besides the police/Security Force recovered an amount of Rs. 9,05,450/- (Rupees nine lakh five thousand four hundred fifty) only in cash from the extremists during the same period. Moreover, during the period, 18 (eighteen) extremists surrendered to the Government Authorities along with four arms which included country made 9 mm pistol, country made .22 pistol, country made AK-56 Rifle, Hand Grenade etc.

Details are as given:

A. Extremists Arrested and Killed (From 1-1-1999 to 31-12-1999)

Organisation	*Arrested No. of persons*	*By Whom*	*Killed No. of persons*	*By Whom*
Valley based	925	(482 by Police/ CRPF, 443 by Army/-AR).	44	(13 by Police/ CRPF, 25 by Army/AR).
Hill based	145	(62 by Police/ CRPF, 83 by Army/AR).	5	(2 by Police/ CRPF, 3 by Army/ AR).
Total	1070	(544 by Police/ CRPF, 526 by Army/AR).	49	(21 by Police CRPF, 28 by Army/AR).

B. Arms and Ammunition Recovered from Extremists (w.e.f. 1-1-1999 to 31-12-1999)

By whom	*Valley Extremists*		*Hill Extremists*		*Total*	
	Arms	*Ammn.*	*Arms.*	*Ammn.*	*Arms*	*Ammn.*
Police/CRPF	76	1802	39	330	115	2132
Army/AR	66	1685	39	1369	105	3054
Total	142	3487	78	1699	220	5186

Remarks

Police/CRPF: The arms include 1 AK-47 Rifle, 3 AK-56 Rifles, 2 Carbines, 1 SLR, 12 9 mm Pistols, 8 (eight) .38 Revolvers, 1 (one) .22 Rifle, 5 M-20 Pistols, 1 (one) .22 Revolvers, 1 Country made Revolver, 5 SBBL Gun, 2 Country made Carbines, 9 Country made Pistols, 1 Rocket Launcher Shell, 1 Remote Control, 1 (one) IED, 4 Bombs and 57 Hand Granades.

Army/AR: The arms include 2 LMG, 3 LMG, 3 AK-47 Rifles, 4 AK-56 Rifles, 7 Sten Carbines, 7 SLR, 1 UMG, 3 M-21 Rifles, 1 USA Carbine, 1 (one) .30 Carbine, 3 (three) .22 Pistols, 6 (six) .38 Revolvers, 1 M-20 Pistol, 5 (five) 9 mm Pistols, 1 (one) .32 Revolver, 1 (one) .22 Revolver, 2 M-16 Rifles, 8 (eight) .303 Rifles, 1 Bolt Action Rifle, 1 (one) .45 Revolver, 1 DBBL Gun, 5 SBBL Guns, 1 Shot Gun, 3 Country made Revolvers, 2 Country made Carbines, 1 Country made AK-47 Rifle, 2 Country made Pistols, 9 Country made Guns, 2 Bombs and 21 Hand Grenades.

C. Money Recovered from Extremists during the Period from 1-1-1999 to 31-12-1999

Amount	*From Whom*	*By Whom*
Rs. 8,06,570.00	Valley Extremists	(Rs. 59,185.00 by Police/CRPF) (Rs. 7,47,385.00 by Army/AR)
Rs. 98,880.00	Hill Extremists	(Rs. 880.00 by Police/CRPF) (Rs. 98,000.00 by Army/AR)
Rs 9,05,450.00		(Rs. 60,065.00 by police/CRPF) (Rs. 8,45,385.00 by Army/AR)

D. Extremists Surrendered to the Govt. Authorities during the period from 1-1-1999 to 31-12-1999

Sl. No.	*Name of Organisation*		*Type of Weapons Surrendered*
1.	PLA	= 3	1-HE 36 Hand Grenade.
2.	UNLF	= 5	2-Country made 9 mm Pistol with live rounds.
3.	PREPAK	= 4	3-W/T Sets.
4.	KCP	= 2	1-Country made .22 Pistol with 5 rounds.
5.	KYKL	= 4	1-AK-56 Rifle with 18 rounds and one Chinese Detonator.
Total		18	

E. Narcotic Drugs/Plants Seized/Destroyed during 1-1-1999 to 31-12-1999

(a) Heroin Powder Seized	: 4 Kgs and 316 milligrams
(b) Ganja Seized	: 151 Kgs
(c) Ganja Plants Destroyed	: 60,000 Plants

F. Total Amount of Fines Levied Under M.V. Act and Police Act during 1-1-1999 to 31-12-1999

(a) M.V. Act	: Rs. 2,63,930/-
(b) Police Act	: Rs. 7,290/-

The Life Line of Manipur, the National Highway No. 39 and 53 are under the control of unlawful organisations. It is a very difficult situation to regain control from them.

But, a National Highways Scheme has been prepared. Police Department envisages better patrolling and telecommunication coverage of both the National Highways No. 39 and 53 to curb extortion and killing on these routes by the militants and antisocials as well as to ensure smooth flow of essential commodities into the state. The scheme, however, is still awaiting clearance from the Central Government.

The general law and order situation in the state, apart from the problem of insurgency and ethnic clash, is also affected by other crimes attracting sanctions of I.P.C. and other Acts. The crime statement of three years as enclosed indicated decrease in the trend of heinous offences like murder etc. which is paradigm of limping back of law and order situation to normalcy.

A. IPC Offences

Sl. No.	*Head of Crime*	*1997*	*1998*	*1999*
1.	Murder	325	210	184
2.	Attempt to Murder	193	131	113
3.	Culpable Homicide not amounting to murder	5	5	6
4.	Dacoity	11	22	19
5.	Robbery	26	18	20
6.	Burglary	109	109	76
7.	Theft	259	270	276
8.	Rioting	75	60	72
9.	Rape	9	13	10
10.	Kidnapping			
	(a) Male	110	68	34
	(b) Female	57	49	42
11.	Cheating	61	44	58
12.	Criminal Breach of Trust	18	12	19
13.	Counterfeiting	4	14	9
14.	Motor Accident	396	410	496
15.	Offence Against State	450	346	284
16.	Assault	221	227	203
17.	Other IPC Cases not included above	733	513	477
Total		3062	2521	2398

B. Minor/Other Local and Special Laws

Sl. No.	*Head of Crime*	*1997*	*1998*	*1999*
1.	Arms Act	36	42	19
2.	Explosive Act	17	27	34
3.	ND & PS Act	181	126	42
4.	PG Act	23	8	4
5.	Excise Act	35	—	—
6.	SITA Act	—	—	—
7.	Foreigners Act	2	—	1
8.	Passport Act	11	9	—
9.	E.C. Act	1	3	—
10.	TDA (P) Act	—	—	—
11.	Cinematography Act	2	11	—
12.	P.C. Act	—	—	—
13.	UA (P) Act	283	403	477
14.	Other Acts not included above	23	14	13
Total		614	643	590

The activities of the various extremist organisations operating in Manipur claimed many lives besides causing loss of a number of arms and ammunition, vehicles etc.

A. Activities of Extremists from 1-1-1999 to 31-12-1999
No. of Security Forces Killed by Extremists

CRPF	*Police*	*BRTF*	*Army/AR*	*Total*
18	12	1	12	43

B. No. of Persons Killed by Extremists and Clash between Themselves

Manipuri	*Non-Manipuri*	*Killing among themselves*	*Excise*	*Surrendary*	*Total*
19	2	7	1	1	30

86 (eighty six) guns were snatched from the Security Forces and Police by the Extremists from different places during the period aforementioned.

Now-a-days, both public and private lives have no security at all as they are unable to protect themselves from the offences of the extremists and there is no way for escape from the clutches of extremists' extortion, kidnapping, witch-hunting, and corruption have become normal practice. There are no political ethics, no concern for the fundamental duties of a citizen, no question of Human

Rights and no question of public opinion. Might rules and gun is the law. It is too difficult to say if our state Government even exists!

Whenever there is
Decline of righteousness,
I incarnate myself
To protect the virtuous
And to destroy the wicked,
From Age to Age.

—Geeta (IV.7/8)

The time and situation invites Central Rule.

REFERENCES

1. Introduction to the Constitution of India: Durga Das Basu.
2. Speeches of Prime Ministers Produced by: Directorate of Advertising and Visual Publicity, Ministry of Information and Broadcasting Government of India.
3. Local Daily Newspapers: particularly Poknapham Manipuri Daily.
4. Manipur Today: Published by DIPR, Govt. of Manipur.

Student Politics in Manipuri Society

M.C. Arun

The present paper is not a comprehensive history of student politics in Manipur. In such a limited paper, it is practically impossible to focus on all the issues taken up by the student bodies in the state and their areas of interest. In this paper, we take up only three major issues. The three issues gave a good input to the entire political system of this state. The issues are (a) secularization of education (b) foreigners issue and (c) language issue. While discussing these issues, many details could not be covered due to lack of space. But, as far as possible, we have tried to highlight the spirit of the issues and the movements.

I

The participation of students in the polity first emerged in the 19th century. The German students body of *Burschenschaft*, founded in 1815, greatly influenced the government in the liberalization of its machineries and unification of the Germans into a single nation. It also worked for elimination of the out of fashion medieval practices in the University, so that, academic freedom in learning and teaching could be attained. Many other student bodies came up in the course of history with different aims and objects since then. Some of them were highly charged with political ideology; while other bodies acted as pressure groups or interest groups with or without a definite political ideology. "By twentieth century, the cumulative experience of generations of fighting students had produced a very high level of political consciousness in Latin American University students. It was they who succeeded in reforming their universities from 1918 onwards to a level which was unsurpassed during the following fifty years in America, Britain, France or Germany"[1]. It was the Cordoba Manifesto of 1918 which gave a impetus towards active participation of students in politics in the twentieth century political scenario of Latin America.

The Cordoba Manifesto was the first declaration on students rights. It "denounced the old administration in which there was no reform of curricula, and no reform of rules, for fear that someone might lose his job because of the change, and it announced: We want to eradicate from university organization the archaic and barbarous concept of authority which in university is a bulwark of absurd tyranny"[2]. The movement soon gained momentum to spread to other South American countries—Peru in 1919, Colombia in 1924, Paraguay in 1927, Brazil and Bolivia in 1928, Mexico in 1929 and Costa Rica in 1930s [3]. All these movements were but legacies of the active political involvement of students in 19th century politics. "Latin American University youth played a leading part in the wars of independence at the beginning of the nineteenth century, and have gone on struggling against tyranny ever since"[4].

Student politics in United States was something quite different. The first Students' Union was established in 1896 at the University of Pennsylvania; but major unions came up only in 1930. "This growth is the result of general acceptance by educators of the concept that leisure-time activities have educational value—that much development of students takes place outside the classroom"[5]. In the 1960s, students started to demand and often get a much larger share in shaping policies. "Notable changes were evident in the scope of the students government. Nearly all US campuses have had for years some form of students government. The chief purpose of students governments were to help the administration maintain effective relations with the students body and to give students direct experience in self-government"[6].

The most radical student group, Students for a Democratic Society (SDS) came into existence in 1960. Thomas E. Hayden, a student of the University of Michigan, published his famous *Port Huron Statement* in 1962. Based on that statement, the SDS declared, "the American political system had failed to achieve social or international peace or end poverty and exploitation, and called for a 'participatory democracy' in which individuals could share in social decisions that directly affect their lives"[7]. The SDS involved itself actively in the Civil Rights movements in its early stage; later, the group was in the forefront of the Anti-Vietnam War movement. It tried to mobilize the blacks, the poor, and the exploited to transform society by revolution and its ideology was direct confrontation with the American capitalist system. As its history went on, "In 1969, SDA split into three factions. The Progressive Labour faction, a pro-Maoist group, tried to divert campus members of SDS away from campus politics towards the working-class movement. The Revolutionary Youth Movement-II sought to transfer the University into an arena of revolutionary action. The Weatherman faction, also known as Revolutionary Youth Movement-I, considered itself the vanguard of violent revolution, with students, workers, and blacks presenting a United Front. They endorsed terrorism as part of an armed struggle and conducted workshops on explosives and sabotage. At its 1972 convention, SDS was clearly controlled by the Progressive Labour faction, doctrinaire and disciplined but opposed to violence"[8].

Many countries of the Third World saw the growth of militant student movements in the early twentieth century. In Cuba (1950s), Czechoslovakia (1968) and China (1919) students played vital roles in changing the then existing political order. In 1933, the students in Cuba "were mainly instrumental in bringing down the Machado dictatorship in alliance with a group of rebellious army sergeants; and under Batista's second dictatorship, 1952–58, they played a leading role in both the urban and the rural resistance movements. In March 1957, they organized an unsuccessful assassination attempt on Batista and several of their leaders were killed; subsequently they participated in sabotage in Havana and many went to the mountains of Oriente to fight with the Rebel Army"[9]. Even after Castro's revolution, the students went on to participate in every sphere of state politics.

The Chinese experience is more interesting in the sense that the student action preceded the Chinese Communist movement. The Peking University, founded in 1898, was the academic centre of the Chinese Revolution. The Peking students staged a gigantic demonstration on 4 May 1919 against Japanese imperialism and its expansion into Manchuria. "In the civil war between the Kuomintang and the Chinese Communist Party, majority of the students opted for Mao Tse-Tung and supported the Chinese Revolution of 1949"[10].

Upto 1925, the students were more powerful than the Party itself. "The first Party secretary, Chen Tu Hsiu, was a professor at Peking University. Mao Tse-Tung himself was initiated into politics through student movements in Peking and Changsha, and one of his first political experiences was a student strike in sympathy with 4 May movement, in June 1919"[11]. The students also took a major role in carrying out Mao's unique Cultural Revolution[12].

The Japanese experience is, however, slightly different from others. The Japanese students started to perform political actions in an organized way in 1960. They moved out against the renewal of the Security Treaty between Japan and US. There were a series of demonstrations over the issue. In addition, there were two equally important issues in 1960s. The three separate issues of the struggle were the resignation of Kishi for his action of 19 May, the cancellation of Eisenhower's visit, and the prevention of the Security Treaty"[13].

But, there were tensions between different student bodies in Japan. The most serious conflict was between the students of Private Universities and those of National Universities. Student politics was, notably, dominated by the National Universities. At the ideological front, though All Japan Federation of Student Self-Government Association swept Japan for about 20 years in post war period, Japanese students started to leave aside the Communist Party in 1955–56. "In 1958, two new organizations were set up which were to exercise a great influence over the students—the Kakukyodo (which was a political organization) and the Shagakudo (which was a purely student body) ... The JCP groups or *anti-mainstream* faction regarded the US as the main target; whereas the mainstream were more concerned with internal Japanese issues and the overthrow of the existing power structure"[14]. In spite of these conflicts, the student movement "has played a historic role in any world perspective. It pioneered mass revolutionary action in an industrialized country, years before it was achieved in Europe and America...it has demonstrated that students can forge effective links with the most oppressed classes in society—workers and peasants"[15].

Student movement in South East Asia was mainly the product of the anti-colonial movements. Though the political consciousness of the students were shaped by the nationalist movements, the students in the region could not develop into a community. This is because of the fact that, there were only a limited number of educational institutions. But, they had been associated "with nascent political elements outside the University community. The students were articulated in discussion groups, youth congresses, women's congresses, and in politically oriented articles published in a variety of newspapers and journals[16].

In Burma, the students had been taking part in political movements since the 1920s. The trouble was started with an announcement of Secretary Montagu in 1917–18. The Montagu-Chelmsfold "recommended that Burma's case should be reserved for special consideration, since her people were of a different race, at a different stage of political development, and with altogether different problems. The storm of protest which suddenly arose in Burma when the nature of the alternative proposals for her political development became known, a storm of protests followed and it took everybody by surprise. Burmese national sentiments flared up to fever pitch"[17]. In the mean time, the opening of University of Rangoon in December, 1920 made room for a widespread student strike at the instigation of the politicians. "Discontent focused on the efforts of the British-appointed University governing agencies to stiffen preparatory standards and to free the University from political interference"[18]. But it was in 1930s that the students could act for a movement of wider perspectives. By 1936, the Rangoon University Student Union (RUSU) became the headquarters of student agitation for entire country. "The aggressive spirit of the student movement owed much to the frustration experienced by the vast majority of students in their efforts to obtain diplomas and suitable employment... The sophisticated atmosphere of the University alienated many of Burma's youth from parental authority. The student movement was, therefore, as much a product of an artificial and ill-adapted educational regiment as it was an expression of the rising tide of political disaffection. Many students developed a genuine interest in contemporary aspects of world affairs and in socialism, which were excluded from the curriculum"[19].

Another force that shaped the student movement is *Dobama Asiayone* (We Burman Association). This Association was formed by amalgamating two national student organizations, the Dobama group and the All Burma Youth League in 1935. The members addressed each other by the term *Thakin* (master) and the Thakin became a symbol of youthful defiance of British rule and an affirmation of faith that Burmans were destined to be masters in their own country. The Thakins were, as a rule, dedicated nationalists, disdainful of fellow students who aspired for entry into the civil services and also hostile to middle-class politicians who mouthed nationalist slogans for the purpose of enhancing their political fortunes"[20].

Though the memorable strike of February 1936 was led by the Rangoon University Student Union, it was precipitated by the Thakin leaders who had won control of the RUSU. History tells that "The Thakin associates in the 1936 strike became the champions of Burmese nationalism against both the British and the Japanese, and they took over the political leadership of independent Burma after 1949"[21].

After the military seizure of power in 1955, RUSU and ABSU acted in alliance with the Burma Communist Party (BCP). Many Karen, Shan and Kachin students left university to fight with their respective insurgent groups against the Burmese Government. This was the beginning of student action in free Burma[22].

In Indonesia, some students who had been educated in Holland were very much conscious of the disparity between colonized and free nations. "In the early 1920s, they consolidated their strength by transforming the then existing Indonesian student organization into a militant organization promoting unity and solidarity among people native to the Indonesian archipelago but stressing exclusiveness with respect to non-Indonesian students. This small but highly active student association, the *Perhimpoenan Indonesia* (Indonesian Association) was one of the first organizations openly to advocate an independent Indonesia"[23].

After the short drama of political powers in 1942–43, the Netherlands transferred the sovereignty on 27 December, 1949. The political scenario of the independent Indonesia was dominated by a political confusion. "President Sukarno became in time an advocate of a centralized program of 'guided democracy' in an endeavour to exploit the revolutionary fervour of Communist partisans, who also opposed particularism and multiparty rule. His *Pantja Sila* ideal included faith in Allah and devotion to nationality, humanity, democracy, and social justice; but the precise meanings were unclear, and implementation was sadly lacking. Sukarno's attempt to bridge the chasm between Islam and communism incurred the inevitable risk that he would alienate both sides and thus compromise the achievement of espoused objectives"[24]. His proposals were strongly objected by the Muslim parties and started the chronic conflict between the Islamic and leftist groups. This had a strong impact on the student politics in 1960s.

The student politics in 1965 was dominated by the conflict between Islamic groups (especially HMI) and leftist groups (CGMI). "On October 25, 1965, a group of representatives from virtually all student associations (the major exceptions being CGMI and two other communist-oriented organizations) acted on the proposal of the Minister of Higher Education and Sciences and formed a new federative student organization. The new organization was called the Indonesian Students' Action Front or *KAMI* .... That the fate of KAMI was more than a manifestation of student indignation at the assassinations carried out by the '30th of September Movement' was revealed in the importance which students attached to the distinction between what they labelled the "older order" and the "new order" toward which they were working. The threefold demands of KAMI hinted at a broad reform orientation: (i) dissolution of the Indonesian Communist Party, (ii) dismissal of cabinet members and formation of a new cabinet, (iii) reduction of prices"[25]. This was starting point of a new beginning of student politics in post independent era of Indonesia.

Indian students entered politics, like many of other colonized countries, with the emerging and growing nationalist movement. "In 1928, a student organization was formed in Punjab under the leadership of Lala Lajpat Rai. In the same year, an All Bengal Students' Association was presided by Jawaharlal Nehru. In 1936 an All India Students' Federation was established... The Congress leaders, in 1945, established... All India Students' Congress. In 1950, this organization was dissolved"[26]. After India got its sovereignty in 1947, student bodies were widely charged with different political ideologies; there are many national and regional (even state-based) student organizations. Some notable national level bodies are All India Students' Federation, Students' Federation of India, National Students' Union of India, Akhil Bharatiya Vidhyarthi Parishad and all of them acted as notable pressure groups in India's political system. Assessing the present student politics, as examined by Babulal Fadia,[27] Philip G. Altbach says, "The student movement had lost its sense of militant unity and ideological purpose... The nationalist fervour of the pre-independence period has been replaced by generally unorganized and sporadic agitation usually aimed at specific grievances". The four grievances are (a) demands by students upon university authorities, (b) student demands upon non-university authorities on issues of special concern, (c) sporadic, generally unorganized, outburst by students only vaguely associated with concrete demands, (d) activities associated with larger political movements in the areas surrounding the school, college or university.

In India, there are different student organizations operating in a single state with regionalism or region based ideology. For example, student politics started in Assam on nationalistic lines during the colonial period. During the pre-independence period, student organizations were affiliated to the political parties. But, after Independence, "a feeling was developed among the students to organize students more on no-party line. The Assam Students' Association which came into existence in September 1959 was organized on non-partisan, non-political and democratic foundation. It came to stand by the larger and collective interests of the student community, endeavoured to solve the problems common to the students of Assam as well as to promote the spirit of culture, literature, sports etc... (But) because of its participation in Refinery movement and Language movement it was branded as partisan and politically motivated. Therefore, there was mounting pressure for the organization of a student union whereby the students of all classes irrespective of language, religion, hills or plains could take a common platform"[28]. The pressure yielded a new students organization, the All Assam Students' Union, came into being in 1967 with a different political colour.

II

The unique geographical condition of Manipur, to a great extent was the main cause of development of her unique culture and tradition. In Manipur, the dominant culture of Meiteis evolved out of a complex process of cultural assimilation and ethnic amalgamation. The process was disturbed by the appearance of the British and the non-local traders in the first quarter of the 20th century. This was overlooked by the Manipuri elite of those days, but the younger generation started looking into the situation and subsequent events with a critical eye. The situation caused a feeling of anger and hatred in the mind of the youths (see N. Sabita Devi, 1985)[29]. R. Constantine discussed the "lingering argument" of the

Manipuri youths, in his *Manipur: Maid of the Mountains* (1981). The nexus of the British and the non-local traders was transformed to an analogous relation of administrators and the traders in the post merger Manipur. The traders play a vital role in Manipur's economy. He narrated how the image of non-local businessmen operates in the body politic. "The picture of economically exploited Manipur is incomplete without the part played by the administration as long as the state was a Union Territory and therefore the direct charge of the Centre. To the Manipuri mind the Mayang trading class have a vested interest in Manipur's economic backwardness. The top officials are also outsiders. While the Mayang businessmen have control over their economy, the Mayangs in the administration wield the executive power. In conjuction, the two provided a perfect milieu of Pre-independence vintage. But, the British pretended to no democratic functioning. Free India is a democracy where people consciously demand the benefits, political as well as economic, of democracy"[30].

Above all, the ever increasing educated youth force remained unemployed and without socio-economic direction. Though some of them indulge in small time business and black marketing, the majority remain passive in their prime time. Their dreams and ambitions remained a psychological agony which led to the development of a sense of alienation in them.

Manipur experienced a mild form of student protest and saw the growth of student politics during the colonial period. The first signs of a collective thinking among the students of Manipur came in the form of Students' Union at the DM College of Imphal, soon after its establishment after the war (WW II). Later, taking up the cue from DM College students, many other student unions came up in other institutions like the Johnstone School, Churachand High School, Ram Lal Paul High School and Tombisana High School. At the state level, a student organization known as the All Manipur Students' Federation came into being in 1946. The organizations were formed by the students belonging to various political parties—Indian National Congress, Communists and Socialists. On 30 October 1946, the body organized a conference at Churachand High School with the basic objective of "Unity of students community of Meiteis, Muslims and of the Hills". The Federation organized five conferences which became a landmark in the student politics of Manipur. The conferences came up with the following demands—(1) establishment of responsible government in Manipur (2) development of Imphal city and rural municipalities (3) free primary education system (4) establishment of new schools and colleges (5) proper facilities for students (6) combine administration of the hill people and the valley people (7) human rights. The Federation could not exist long, because of its internal conflicts and contradictions.

III

The All Manipur Students' Union (AMSU) came into being in 1965 following a bloody confrontation on 27 August 1965, when police fired upon students protesting against artificial scarcity of rice and killed four persons, and injured many others. The students used the term 'Manipur' and not 'Manipuri' to cover all the students in Manipur irrespective of their place of origin, religion, ethnic affiliation and linguistic identity. For the first time in the history of Manipur, the students were able to form an organisation, free from any political affiliation, dedicated to the welfare of the students and the people in general. However, AMSU did not shy away from political issues right from its early days. The demand for grant of statehood for Manipur was one which the Union took up in 1968. The Union organized several demonstrations, rallies and other forms of protests and it became the focal point of the Statehood movement and indeed, the students under the leadership of AMSU was the mainstay of the prolonged movement.

The year 1972 brought statehood to Manipur. Since then, AMSU began taking up a series of issues which include among others, the movement for doing away with religious functions in educational institutions and anti-foreigners movement.

Secular Ethos

It all started with the celebration of Saraswati Puja in the schools and colleges and collection of fees for the same from the students. AMSU took up the issue and launched a major movement in 1978 and the Government of Manipur finally had to ban the celebration of Saraswati Puja in all the institutions of the state. Saraswati Puja was the most popular celebration of student community in Manipur in the 1950s and 1960s. The celebrations continued for even three or four days and classes came to a halt. It was during the presidentship (AMSU) of Khangembam Cha Kuleswar, that the issue was first brought up. AMSU's basic arguement was that, Manipur being a part of secular India, should not encourage religious functions in the educational institutions. At a meeting of AMSU held on 15 February 1978 at the Manipur College the student community resolved among other things (1) to check frequent religious holidays in schools and (2) to resist collection of fees with regard to religious functions. Accordingly on 3 March 1978, a memorandum was submitted to the Chief Minister of Manipur, alongwith a charter of demands viz., (1) correction of the wrong History of Manipur and the teaching of corrected history of Manipur upto Class X; (2) establishment of a full fledged University in Manipur; (3) Instruction in Meitei script and inclusion of Manipuri language in the Schedule VIII to the Constitution; (4) Abolition of religious functions from educational institutions (abolition of subscription for Puja etc., holiday on religious functions should be stopped except Sunday)...

The students started boycotting Saraswati Puja celebrations all over the state, in pursuant to a resolution of the AMSU Executive Council adopted on 15 February 1978. The State authorities tried to suppress the movement by using the police. They even collected the signatures of the parents of students declaring that they would prevent their wards from participating in any strike.

The movement was intensified in the month of August 1978, after the ultimatum given by AMSU expired. The Union began organising a series of mass demonstrations in the greater Imphal area. On 18 August, a group of about 450 students gathered at the gate of the Chief Minster's bungalow shouting their demands. It was repeated on 23 August and picketed the Chief Minister's office. When four representatives of AMSU met Yangmaso Shaiza, the then Chief Minister, no solution could be reached. Then, violent activities followed. On 28 August, AMSU staged another procession of about 500 students from different parts of greater Imphal. Thirty three students were arrested in that connection. The police unable to control the students resorted to firing on the demonstrators. Luckily no one was seriously injured in the police firing. A press note of AMSU issued the next day flayed the police action and termed it as a sign of inefficiency. It asked— "Why should the students be fired upon, when all they were asking was that they should be taught the true history of Manipur, that no Puja should be compulsory in educational institutions, that their own script should be taught, that a full-fledged university should be established, that the price of essential commodities should be brought down?" It further added, "where is our freedom when we are fired upon only because we like our true history lessons, secularism and our own script?"

The state government issued a clarification on the police firing, which said "...there was no other alternative as number of students who joined the demonstrators multiplied that day. About one thousand students of schools and colleges staged a lone procession in front of the New Secretariat building, Government of Manipur. They shouted their slogans and demanded to release the arrested students. Another group of about 500 students also approached the spot from the southern direction. The Manipur Rifles personnel tried to stop them on the way. There was confusion in the situation among the security personnel. When some students tried to set on fire a petrol tank, police opened fire at 2.30 pm. Angry students pelted stones... That day eleven students were arrested on the spot. Nobody was reportedly injured, however, in the firing..."

On 31 August 1978, the state government announced certain steps to be taken up in response to the demands of AMSU. The steps were:

(1) Correction of the wrong history of Manipur and corrected history would be introduced upto class X. The Press Note further informed that three scholars have been appointed to examine the lesson in history of Manipur, then taught in the schools of Manipur. The scholars are expected to submit their report within 3 months. The government also agreed to consider the recommendation of the scholars and make necessary changes in the syllabi as it considered necessary.

(2) In relation to the instruction of Meitei script of Government informed that it had already invited applications for the post of two research fellows and submit their findings regarding the correct versions of the old script. Another important additional point which the government made was its assurance that it "will make efforts to adopt the universally accepted Manipuri script." It promised that the appointment of scholars would be made by 31 October, 1978.

(3) Regarding the abolition of religious functions from educational institutions (abolition of subscription for Puja etc., holidays on

religious functions should be stopped except Sunday). The Government informed that the Constitution of India assured freedom of worship as one of the Fundamental Rights. It therefore said that "demands for not granting holidays for religious functions and worship would be unconstitutional. However, regarding the collection of subscription, it stated that it did not neither issue 'orders' for collection of any type of subscription for any religious functions nor ask any college to hold any religious function."

On September 7, AMSU and the government signed an agreement consisting of four points: (i) introduction of Meitei script and inclusion of Manipuri language in the Schedule VIII to the Indian Constitution; (ii) abolition of religious functions from educational institutions; (iii) adoption of one village by each college for undertaking development; (iv) the establishment of an Engineering college in Manipur State.

The Outsiders' Threat

Another movement of AMSU which shook the state for quite sometime was the anti-foreigners agitation in 1980. The year 1980 also witnessed the splitting up of AMSU into two factions due to its own internal contradictions. One faction was led by Mr. M. Khelen as president and another by Mr. L. Dilip. The two factions did not differ much on the enormity of the threat posed by the 'outsiders'. Both were alarmed with the disproportionate increase of Nepalese, Bengali Muslim population in Manipur during the 1951–1971 period and they dreaded a repeat performance of Tripura where the indigenous Tripuris were reduced to a pitiable minority in their own ancestral land by the Bengalis.

A booklet of AMSU (Dilip faction) and All Manipuri Students Co-ordinating Committee (AMSCOC) said, "The problem of influx of immigrants into the north eastern region is a national problem. Laudable efforts to safeguard our constitution through deletion of the foreigners from the electoral rolls has been misrepresented as communal or chaotic agitation. As a result the movement to preserve the identity and ethos of Manipuris has been misrepresented. This movement is the struggle of Manipuris to save their home and hearth from a silent civilian invasion by herds of illegal immigrants from Bangladesh, Nepal and Burma.

Another leaflet circulated by the AMSU (Khelen faction) declared— "Those persons who do not like the death of Manipuris in the hands of the ever increasing foreigners should agree to the AMSU's stand and join the fight against the foreigners."

AMSU was not the first to raise the issue of foreigners. It was the Kuki National Assembly which first brought the issue to people's attention and subsequently followed up by AMSU, during the presidentship of Khomdram Dorendra in 1972–73. The Kuki National Assembly, Manipur whose demand was the deletion of Nepalese voters from the electoral rolls, entered into an agreement with the then United Legislative Party Government, headed by Md. Alimuddin on 1 August, 1972. No action was followed up since the date of the Agreement.

In 1980, the anti-foreigners agitation became a mass movement, although the people were at times disillusioned by the rivalry between the two factions, although their demands on the foreigners issue was more or less the same. The demand of AMSCOC according to a memorandum submitted to the government of Manipur on 15 February, 1980 was removal of illegal immigrants from the electoral roll and their deportation from Manipur. The stand of AMSU (Dilip faction) was also on the same lines, as reflected in the resolution taken in a general body meeting held on 7 March, 1980. Besides the demand for checking influx and deletion, the Khelen faction put in a demand for reintroduction of the Inner Line Permit System.

The AMSU agitators organised several demonstrations in Imphal area. The students even went to the extent of shouting slogans and distributing pamphlets even inside the State Legislative Assembly Hall on 18 March 1980 during the assembly session. Six students were apprehended by the security personnel on that day. The movement was intensified with mass awareness programs through leaflets, pamphlets, booklets and public meetings. They also boycotted regular classes and even examinations. Demonstrations and picketing of government offices followed.

On 25 March, the Khelen faction decided to boycott the important High School Leaving Certificate Examination 1980 scheduled to begin on 17 April that year. The Dilip faction and AMSCOC also took a similar decision. However, the Khelen faction withdrew its boycott call on 28 March, as the Government agreed to consider its demands. The other group AMSU (Dilip) and AMSCOC reaffirmed its boycott call of the HSLC examination on

14 April with another decision to prevent holding of other examinations as well.

On 17 April, the examination was disturbed by the students at different places. They snatched away admit cards, answer scripts from the examinees and even threatened the teachers. When some of them tried to boycott the conduct of the examination at Lilashing Khongnangkhong High School, a locality on the northern side of Imphal, CRPF personnel on duty opened fire to control the protestors. Mr. P. Premananda alias Lukhoi, aged about 18 years, died on the spot. Mr. N. Somorendra Singh was wounded in the firing. Next day, after the morning shift of the examination, in the premises of Leiren Girls' High School, Nambol (a town about 16 kms away from Imphal), a group of about six students snatched the answer scripts and torched them. Manipur Rifles personnel opened fire; and in the incident one student, Mr. Huidrom Lokendra, aged about 23 of Ishok village was killed.

Following these incidents, the examination was postponed indefinitely. And the state government began parleys with the representatives of different political parties and some special invitees on 10 April on the issue. The Chief Minister R.K. Dorendra invited the Presidents and the General Secretaries of CPI, CPM, Congress (I), Congress (U), MPP, KNA, Lok Dal, Janata Party, Ireipak Leishem Party, leaders of both factions of AMSU and a few special invitees namely N.K. Sanajaoba, O. Bhogendro, A. Somorendra and Th. Tarunkumar. A state level committee was formed to confer with the Central Government so that a solution be reached on or before 25 April, 1980. But the Chief Minister Dorendra's appeal to agitating Assam students to accept 1971 as base year of identification of foreigners in Assam disturbed the game-plan.

The stalling of talks led to the Khelen faction changing its agitation mode and began raiding the godowns of non-Manipuri businessmen for hoarding essential commodities and artificial price rise. They forcibly seized the essential commodities and distributed the same to the public free of cost. In the course of these activities, two students, Mr. Konsam Imoba, aged about 18 years, of Khagempalli and Mr. Thokchom Naba, aged about 18 years, of Nganappithong, died by drowning in the Imphal River while they were trying to escape from a police patrolling party on 30 April, 1980.

After a long and protracted negotiation, the AMSU faction led by Dilip Meetei along with AMSCOC signed an agreement with the state government on 5 August 1980. The Khelen faction failed to reach an agreement with the state Government as its demand for inclusion of a representative of the Central Government as one of the signatories was not agreed to. But the implementation part did not come as expected and it soon became a non-issue due to the loss of public confidence towards the student leaders.

The foreigner issue once again came up in the year 1994 during President's Rule with Mr. N. Mohilal, President AMSU demanding implementation of the agreement signed on 5 August 1980. After a brief agitation, AMSU signed an agreement with the Government of Manipur on 9 November, 1994. Mr. N. Mohilal signed on behalf of AMSU and Mr. K.K. Sethi, Chief Secretary represented the Government of Manipur. Mr. Yambem Laba and Mr. H.V. Goswami, Advisor to Governor signed as witnesses. A Committee was later, formed to identify the foreigners in Manipur. The Committee consisted of three members: Chief Secretary as Chairperson, Home Secretary as Convenor, Under Secretary (Home) as Office Assistant, Mr. Arambam Somorendra and Brajakumar Sharma.

Cultural Identity

The demand for inclusion of Manipuri language in the Schedule VIII of the Indian Constitution was on AMSU's agenda since the late seventies, but somehow it remained as a side issue as AMSU was directing its energies more on the political and economic issues. It was a demand first put forward by the Manipur Sahitya Parishad in the 50s, but it remained as a cultural demand. It was only in the late eighties that the language issue was brought in the forefront of AMSU's demands. As AMSU lended its muscle to the demand, it became a political issue and a people's movement.

In a joint meeting held on 15 March, 1989, in the premises of D.M. College of Science, the language issue was much emphasized and it took a resolution to mobilize the mass to this effect. Mr. Y. Priyokumar, President, AMSU sent a letter to the Prime Minister of India, on 15 May, 1989 demanding the inclusion of Manipuri language in the Schedule VIII. In the letter, he noted that "Manipuri language may be compared with the scheduled languages... as follows:

1. Mother tongue of the majority of the population in concerned state;

2. Official language of the concerned state;
3. Language of the Courts other than the High Court;
4. Primary medium of broadcast of All India Radio Programme;
5. Vehicle of an advanced and developed literature;
6. Medium of instruction and examination from primary to post graduate level.

In 1990, the language demand was primarily focused alongwith other equally weighted demands, viz., (1) Removal of Armed Forces (a) (Assam and Manipur) Special Power Act, 1958 and (b) Extension of Manipur Land Revenue and·Land Reforms Act, 1960 to the hill areas of Manipur. The then President Mr. L. Gojendra and his executive Council took the resolution for the language demand and removal of the Act of 1958, among others on the AMSU's annual celebration of Hunger Marchers Day, on 27 August 1989.

More and more cultural organizations joined in. From 12 December 1990, AMSU started a campaign for using Meitei archaic characters on the posters, sign-boards in Imphal; later the campaign was extended to other areas of the state (specially in the valley region). For the first time, political parties and candidates began to use Manipuri script in election posters in the Parliamentary and Assembly Election of 1989, 1990. AMSU also took signatures from the candidates of Assembly Election promising that they would resign if Manipuri language was not included in the Schedule VIII and if the Act of 1960 was not extended to the hill areas of the state. Only the Congress (I) candidates refused to sign up.

The language movement was intensified by AMSU in 1992. Besides protests and demonstrations, AMSU boycotted National Papers, Hindi films and songs. Mr. S. Saratchandra, the then President of AMSU was a member of Language Demand Coordinating Committee which was formed by liked minded cultural bodies. At last, the Government of India conceded to the demand and passed a constitutional amendment including Manipuri language in the VIII Schedule of the Indian Constitution on 21 August, 1992.

IV

In conclusion, we would like to say that AMSU, representing the youth and student power of the state, has always worked for betterment of the Manipuri society. The social interests at the collective level are becoming the political interests of AMSU. The social interests that have permanent effect on the society, to a large extent, are readily taken up by them. AMSU so far has shown itself as the champion of political agitation. They draw their strength from the people.

REFERENCES

1. Paloczi-Horath, George 1971. *Youth Up in Arms*, Weidenfeld & Nicolson, p. 184.
2. Cocknurn, Alexander & Robin Blackburn (eds.) 1969. *Student Power*, Penguin, pp. 288–289.
3. Halliday, Fred "Students of the World Unite" in ibid. p. 289.
4. Paloczi-Horath, George op. cit. p. 183.
5. *Encyclopedia Americana,* vol. 7, p. 255.
6. Ibid., p. 254.
7. Ibid., vol. 25, p. 809.
8. Ibid.
9. Paloczi-Horath, George op. cit., p. 293.
10. "Student Movement" in *Lexicon Universal Enclopedia*, vol 18, p. 307.
11. Halliday in Cockburn, op. cit., p. 299.
12. "Chinese Communist Youth League" in *China Quarterly*, October–December, 1962.
13. Halliday in Cockburn, op. cit., pp. 296–97.
14. Ibid., pp. 295–296.
15. Ibid., p. 298.
16. Douglas, Stephen A. & Harsja Backtiar "Indonesian Students: Generation of 1966" in Altbach, Philip 1970. *The Student Revolution: A Global Analysis*, Lalvani, p. 158.
17. Hall, D.G.E. 1968. *A History of South East Asia*, Mcmillan, p. 740.
18. Cady, John F. 1976. *South East Asia: its historical development*, Tata Mcgraw, p. 509.
19. Ibid., p. 521.
20. Ibid.
21. Ibid., p. 522.
22. See Silverstein, Joself "Burmese Student Politics in Changing Society" in Altbach, op. cit.
23. Stephen et al., op. cit., p. 158.
24. Cady, op. cit., p. 600; see also Hall, pp. 833–839.
25. Stephen, op. cit., p. 161.
26. Fadia, Babulal 1980. *Pressure Groups in Indian Politics*, Radiant, p. 61.
27. Ibid., pp. 61–62.
28. Barua, Indrani 1990. *Pressure Groups in Assam*, Omsons, p. 20.
29. See N. Sabita 1985. *An Enquiry into the Revolutionary Activities of Manipuri Youth during the period 1979–83*, an M.Phil. dissertation to Gandhigram Rural Institution, Madurai (unpublished).
30. R. Constatine 1981. *Manipur: Maid of the Mountains*, Lancers p. 98.

Problem of Unemployment among the Educated Youth in Manipur

M. Amarjeet Singh

The paper reports on the expansion of education in Manipur, and notes the alarming rise of unemployment among the educated youth as revealed by the Employment Exchange Statistics. It analyses as well the possible consequences of youth unemployment on the Manipuri society and the problems generally faced by most of the educated youth.

Introduction

It is difficult to accurately assign lower and upper age limits for youth. Because, this vary from time to time, and also from society to society. The United Nations identifies the age between 15–24 as "Youth" which has been adopted in many countries of the West. Whereas in India the age between 15–34 is recognised as youth (*Saraswathi*, 1988). The period of youth stands for growth, development, action and leadership. They mature quickly in an atmosphere where there is freedom, activity, recognition and opportunity. Problems associated with youth are part of the problems that the society as a whole faces. If their energy is channeled constructively it yields to delightful future, not only for them, but also for the society as a whole. Today, youth is confronted with problems and issues, affecting them and their society. Among them, unemployment among the youth in general and educated unemployment in particular is most significant. Unemployment, is one of the most serious problems facing the developing countries like India. It affects individuals, families and communities in many different ways. It can be simply defined as a state of being without gainful work. It is also considered as an involuntary failure to get income yielding work. Unemployment is a condition of one who is able to work but unable to find it (*Harris and Levely*, 1975).

Therefore, an unemployed person is one who has potentialities and willingness to earn or work, but is unable to find a remunerative work. It should be noted that unemployment has three elements:

(1) the individual should be capable of working;
(2) the individual should be willing to work; and
(3) the individual must make an effort to find a remunerative work.

It is a major source of hardship, deprivation and suffering to many people. Whereas, employment very much determines one's chances for leading a peaceful and meaningful life. Our action, feeling and thought are also very much influenced by it. An individual status in the family as well as in the community is also shaped and influenced by the employment he or she holds. Now, let's look at the three aspects of employment as given by *Amartya Sen* (1975):

(1) *the income aspect*: employment gives an income to the employed;
(2) *the production aspect*: employment yields an output; and
(3) *the recognition aspect*: employment gives a person the recognition of being engaged in something.

Development of Modern Education in Manipur

Modern education in Manipur was brought by the Britishers. Though, it has made little progress during the colonial period. In the beginning of the 19th Century a school was established with great effort by George Gordon, but lasted for about a year only because of the absence of public response. In 1872, W.E. Nuthall, the then political agent, opened a school at Imphal, but the school also could not last long. Sir James Johnstone, who was in Manipur as political agent during 1877–86, with king's approval established an English School at Imphal in 1885. Again in 1894, William Pettigrew, an English Missionary started a school at Imphal. But within some months, the authorities decided against the continuation of the school because of his evangelization. Though, Pettigrew was permitted to work among the Tangkhul Nagas and chose Ukhrul as the Mission Centre. By the end of 1897, there were only one Middle

English School and four Lower Primary schools in Manipur. A girl school was started at Imphal in 1899. In 1902, the number of schools in the valley rose to 18 with a total enrollment of 1450. Till 1921, there were no highschools in Manipur, so, many students could not continue their secondary education. But in 1921. Johnstone M.E. School was upgraded to high school level. And in 1936, there were altogether 60 schools in Manipur. The first college was established in 1946. After the independence of India, education made rapid progress in Manipur. There were 455 primary schools, 82 secondary schools and one college in 1951. Table 1 shows the growth of educational institutions in Manipur in some selected years.

Table 1. Growth of Educational Institutions, Manipur.

Year	*Universities*	*College for Gen. Education*	*High/ Higher Sec. Schools*	*Middle/ Senior Basic Schools*	*Pre-Primary/ Primary Schools*
1955–56	–	2	23	87	878
1965–66	–	11	118	299	2077
1975–76	–	20	212	432	3463
1985–86	1	28	358	440	2679
1995–96	2	50	539	535	2448
1997–98	2	50	576	611	2548

Source: *Statistical Handbook of Manipur*, 1992.
Statistical Abstract of Manipur, 1998.

There has been a considerable expansion of educational institutions since independence. During 1955–56, there were just 2 colleges for general education, whereas during 1955–56 the number of colleges rose to 11, 20 in 1975–76, 28 in 1985–86 and 50 in 1997–98. At present the state has 67 colleges including 9 professional colleges/institutes (Medicine—1, Law—2, Teacher Education—2, Fine Art—1, Physical Education—1, Engineering/Technology—2). In 1955–56, there were altogether 988 schools in the state as compared to 3,785 in 1997–98, an almost four times in almost four decades. Before the establishment of Manipur University in 1980, there was a Post-Graduate centre of Jawaharlal Nehru University, Delhi in Imphal. There is a Central Agricultural University in the state, which provides research and instruction on agriculture and related aspects.

Along with the increase in the number of educational institutions, there has been considerable expansion of student enrolment in the state. During 1955–56 the number of students enrolled in schools was 86,502 as against 5,27,789 in 1997–98. The enrolment of students in colleges for general education was only 1,194 in 1955–56 which rose to 17,857 in 1997–98. Again, there were 6,770 students enrolled in colleges for professional education in the state during 1996–97. Table 2 presents the enrolment of students from 1955–56 to 1995–96 at ten yearly interval, and during 1997–98 in the state.

Table 2. Enrolment of Students, Manipur

Year	*Pre-Primary/ Primary Jr. Basic Schools*	*Middle/ Senior Basic Schools*	*High/Higher Sec. Schools*	*College for Gen. Edn.*	*Post-Graduation*
1955–56	66,510	9,169	9,823	1,94	—
1965–66	1,32,856	38,744	35,417	5,797	—
1975–76	2,03,845	50,240	58,845	16,604	—
1985–86	1,73,602	67,143	1,05,846	24,467	1,065
1995–96	2,32,179	1,03,228	1,64,021	—	1,272
1997–98	1,77,099	1,29,663	2,21,027	17,857	—

Source: *Statistical Abstract of Manipur*, 1998.

Because of the rapid expansion of educational institutions and enrolment, the percentage of literacy in the state has also risen. In the beginning of the twentieth century (1901) the percentage of literacy was less than one per cent, which rose to 59.9 per cent in 1991, against all India figure of 52.21 per cent. So far, Imphal district (now Imphal East and Imphal West districts) recorded the highest rate of literacy (70.7 per cent) in the state.

Magnitude of Unemployment among the Educated Youth in Manipur

Manipur, is a small and an economically backward state, with a per-capita income (at 1980–81 prices) of Rs. 2,155 in 1997–98. Agriculture and its allied activities are the main occupation of the people in the state. According to 1991 census, the work-force participation ratio of Manipur is 38.6 per cent, out of which 68 per cent are engaged in primary sectors, and the rest i.e. 32 per cent in secondary and tertiary sectors. The state though endowed with rich resources both natural as well as human, has remained one of the most backward state in the country due to the lack of adequate infrastructure like power, transport and communication, skilled labour, shortage of capital and low level of credit facilities etc. Again, the state shows wide regional disparities in terms of infrastructural facilities. The valley areas being comparatively more developed than the hill areas.

Industrialization in the state has taken place at a very low pace. There is absence of large and medium scale industries, which can provide employment opportunities in large number. Though, the industrialization emphasis in the state is given in the development of small scale and cottage industries such as handloom, handicrafts and sericulture keeping in view of their potential for employment generation. The state is also giving emphasis on various self-employment schemes like Prime Minister's Rozgar Yojana (PMRY). However, such policies have not yielded the expected result so far. In such a situation, the state is not in a position to give gainful employment to its large army of educated youth. Though, the state is experiencing the rapid expansion of education but its educated youth have become the worst victim of the present educational system.

There has been an alarming rise of educated unemployment in the state. Out of the total unemployment mass prevailing in the state, educated unemployment forms a major part. During 1960–61, there were altogether 10,639 job seekers on the live registers of Employment Exchanges in the state, the figure rose to 1,15,546 in 1980–81, 1,83,495 in 1990–91 and 3,22,253 in 1997–98. If we look at the figure provided by the Directorate of Employment, Imphal there were 3,87,276 job seekers as on 31-12-1999, on live register of Employment Exchanges in the state, out of which 1,29,443 are under-matric and 2,57,883 are matriculate and above. The number of registration, placement offered and total number of job seekers on the live register of Employment Exchanges in some selected years are given in the Table 3.

Now it is clear from the above table that the number of job seekers in the state keep on increasing year after year, whereas the placement effected is very low. There is a large imbalance between the registration and placement done, as it can be seen in the above table also. Again, Table 4 shows the estimated number of educated unemployed on the live register of Employment Exchange in the state.

It is not surprising that for 18 posts advertised by the State Public Service Commission, there were 2,183 applicants in 1990–91 and again in 1994–95, for 20 posts, 3550 candidates made application. Table 5 clearly shows the number of posts advertised and candidates

Table 3. Registration, Placement and Job-seekers on the Live Register

Year	*Registration*	*Placement*	*Jobseekers on the live Register*
1980–81	21,272	703	1,15,546
1985–86	44,510	402	1,37,179
1990–91	33,453	242	1,83,495
1991–92	20,310	174	1,98,148
1992–93	18,455	310	2,15,677
1993–94	29,894	1,390	2,41,272
1994–95	19,189	1,085	2,49,910
1995–96	30,135	143	2,76,157
1996–97	28,189	579	2,99,881
1997–98	31,007	429	3,22,253

Source: *Statistical Handbook of Manipur*, 1992.
Statistical Abstract of Manipur, 1998.

Table 4. Estimated Number of Educated Unemployed, Manipur

Educational Level	*1994*	*1996*	*1998*
Matriculates	1,01,497	1,18,535	1,51,224
Under-Graduate	34,415	40,795	57,801
Graduate & Above	32,479	32,363	48,809
Total Educated	1,68,391	1,91,693	2,57,834

Source: *Compiled from the figure provided by the Directorate of Employment*, Imphal.

Table 5. Number of Posts Advertised and Candidates Recommended by Manipur Public Service Commission, Imphal

Year	*No. of Advertised*	*No. of Applicant*	*Candidates Interviewed*	*Candidates Recommended*
1972–73	35	211	102	32
1975–76	141	1,756	432	111
1980–81	451	3,385	920	361
1985–86	154	9,695	611	145
1990–91	18	2,133	100	30
1991–92	30	673	1	1
1993–94	25	487	17	3
1995–96	—	—	—	—
1996–97	4	84	11	4
1997–98 (Upto Nov. 97)	306	685	16	3

Source: *Manipur Public Service Commission*, Imphal

recommended by Manipur Public Service Commission, Imphal and candidates applied in some selected years.

Problems Associated With Unemployment

The state is badly affected by unemployment in general and unemployment among the educated youth in particular. Educated unemployment is one of the most serious problem facing the state today. Unemployment affects individuals, families and societies in many different ways. It badly affects the youth today, which may prove detrimental to the state. It is worthmentioning what Puttaswamiah have said about unemployment. *Unemployment frustrates an individual and is a stumbling block for the development of the country. It is a great evil, it is a poison, it pollutes the society and wrecks the political fibre of a country. It creates devils, it turns good into bad, it changes an honest worker into a criminal. It encourages dishonesty, patronize corruption, glorifies falsehood, bring out dark side of the human character (Puttaswamiah, 1971).*

Widespread educated unemployment is a cause of concern to everyone. Every year thousands of educated comes out from different educational institutions in and outside the state. But most of them do not get gainful employment. This really implies an enormous waste of human and material resources. Unemployed may turn the youth into a caricature of himself giving the appearance of being stupid, lazy, helpless and non-concern for the future. It may as well result in lowering of goals and aims, which may lead to a distance from society. Interaction with people decreases and normal social life is disturbed. It may also result to late marriage. Unemployed youth are worried, helpless and a frustrated lot because they are not in a position to fulfil their family's and societal expectations and obligations.

Again, the phenomenon of widespread educated unemployment can also be identified by inferior jobs, low income and low social status. For instance, in Manipur, rising unemployment has forced the youth, many of them graduates into pulling rickshaws. But, they mask their faces out of shame (The Telegraph, 5 June, 1997). Hundreds of helpless educated youth, and many of them with post-graduate degrees are teaching in Private Schools, where they are paid a nominal sum as remuneration. Unemployment is also associated with the loss of social status. An educated person is always respected and honored by the people and they are supposed to contribute something for the society. But when the young unemployed fail to play their due roles in the society, they are bound to loose the status once they are accorded to held.

Unemployment also very much affects the family of the unemployed youth economically, socially and psychologically. As an educated person is expected to contribute something for the whole family; but when they fail in fulfilling the family expectation, they develop a feeling of guilt, helplessness and loss of self-confidence. Thus, they are frustrated, and the atmosphere at the level of the family is also disturbed. These youth also face financial hardship and do not feel free to ask for money from their parents any longer. In due course of time, they fail to adjust with the family which affect cordial relationship in the family. Studies have provided that a higher rate of troubles and conflict is found in the family of unemployed. Lastly, unemployment is also to some extent responsible for the loss of family status. Unemployment, not only disturbs individual and family but it also affects the whole society. Widespread unemployment is a great societal loss. It results to loss in production and national wealth and deterioration of the skill, physique and morale of the unemployed labour force. The other devastating effect of unemployment in the society is the increase in criminal and other anti-social activities. The deviant behaviour, crimes and even suicide are likely to accelerate because of unemployment. An inquiry based on police record reports that it is the educated unemployed who have committed more number of crimes than any other category of human beings (Eenadu, 20 May, 1984). Unemployment among the educated youth may increase the risk of alcoholism and drug-addiction in the present Manipuri society.

Lastly, most of the educated unemployed youth are confronted with problems, such as:

a) Financial problems;
b) Psychological problems like, frustration, loss of self-confidence, anxiety;
c) Problem of adjustment with family and also with society;
d) Discouragement by society;
e) Gradual loss of support and trust of the family;
f) Problem related to sex and marriage; and
g) Problem related to identity formation.

Conclusion

Unemployment among the educated youth is widespread in Manipur. There is no satisfactory relation between education and employment in Manipur. It badly affects the present Manipuri youth and the state as a whole. There cannot be social and political stability in the state, if its youth are without work and thus remain unemployed. The policy planners have an urgent responsibility to devise policies that may alleviate this problem and to find out lasting solutions to unemployment. And the youth, particularly the educated youth, should be well prepared to be a job-provider rather than a job seeker.

REFERENCES

Devi, Jamini (1989). *Education in Manipur*, Rai Pravina Press, Imphal.

Government of Manipur, Directorate of Economics & Statistics (1998). *Economic Review,1994–95*, Imphal.

Government of Manipur, Directorate of Economics & Statistics (1993). *Statistical Handbook of Manipur,1992*, Imphal.

Government of Manipur, Directorate of Economics & Statistics (1999). *Statistical Abstract of Manipur,1998*, Imphal.

Harris, W.H. & Levenly, J.S. (1975). *The New Columbia Encyclopaedia*, Columbia University Press, New York.

Puttaswamiah (1971). *Unemployment in India: Policy for Manpower*, Oxford University Press, New Delhi.

Saraswathi, Y. (1988). *Youth in India*, Indian Council of Social Sciences Research, New Delhi.

Sen, Amartya (1975). *Employment, Technology and Development*, Oxford University Press, Delhi.

Wright, W.E. (1938). *The Unemployed Man: A Social Study*, Nisbet, London.

Drug Abuse and AIDS Menace in Manipur

Prof. Ng. Brajachand Singh

Manipur has a geographical area of 22,327 km^2. It is bounded by Nagaland in the north, Mizoram in the south, Assam in the west and Myanmar in the east with 358 km of international border. There are nine districts in the state with 1,837,119 population (1991 census) and male female ratio is 1,000:961 in the state with 61% literacy rate. There are many tribes and the two main tribes are Kukis and Nagas which contribute 35% population of Manipur.

The state has a long international border with Myanmar covering 3 districts namely Churachandpur, Chandel and Ukhrul. The international border is about 300 km long mostly hilly terrain except a few places where district roads exist. Moreh is the most conspicuous of all border towns in Manipur and is the main transit point with Myanmar. Moreh is 94 km away from Imphal and is well connected by roads and is served by regular bus services. The literacy rate is around 60–65%.

Illegal drug trafficking is prevalent in Manipur since 1970. While in 1981, 73% drug abusers used morphine and/or pethidine by intravenous route, in 1983, heroin became the drug of choice for abuse.

Heroin (known as No. 4) is a water soluble powder produced from morphine by a simple chemical process. South East Asia and South West Asia are the traditional areas for production of opium and manufacture of heroin. In South East Asia, Myanmar, Thailand and Laos are notoriously known as the "Golden Triangle". It takes ten kilos of opium to make one kilo of morphine, out of which an equal amount of heroin can be derived. The production of heroin in the "Golden Triangle" started increasing following the Crackdown on the Mexican Centres in late 70s and by 1986, it accounted for over 20% of the U.S.A. market. One of the interesting aspects of drug trafficking is the "Fallout" on route. Hence Russia and China which donot produce heroin reported cases of addiction, when their territory was used as transit points. Therefore, it seems quite natural that Manipur, which has a free border with Myanmar would be supplied with pure heroin. The feeling of detachment, of pleasure in heroin addicts generally lasts for 6–8 hours. Therefore, after every 6 to 8 hours there is an intense craving for the drug, initiating marked withdrawal symptoms in chronic addicts. The cost of heroin increases depending on the distance from the source of manufacture. As a result, the chances of impurity also increases with the distance. The pure heroin can be taken in both injectable form (also known as "fixing") and by smoking or "chasing", whereas the impure form (brown sugar) can be just smoked or "chased".

In the late 70s, a major form of addiction in Manipur was mild tranquillizers and methaqualone. Injectable morphine and pethidine were next in use. Even in 1982, only 1% of the addict in Manipur used to smoke heroin. Gradually, heroin substituted for other psychoactive drugs.

Heroin is sold in packets of different sizes costing between Rs. 20 and 50, or, more per dose.

Heroin by intravenous route is the most commonly used drug amongst IDUs in Manipur. Other drugs in use in Manipur are alcohol, dextropropoxyphene, nitrazepam, cough syrup, buprenorphine, opium and pentazocine. According to a study conducted by voluntary Health Association of India, Manipur Branch during 1992, there were about 40,000 heroin addicts in Manipur. An estimated 72% of drug addicts in the state are IDUs and 95% of them are between 15–35 years of age with needle sharing habits. Manipur, being geographically close to the Golden Triangle where 20% of world's heroin is produced is an alternate route for illegal international drug trafficking, resulting in easy availability of heroin of good quality at cheap rate. The first case of HIV infection in Manipur was detected in October 1989 (officially reported in February 1990) in an injecting drug user.

Since then it has been risen rapidly and reached an alarming epidemic proportion. As on May, 2000 a total of 68,448 persons were screened resulting in the detection of 10,065 HIV seropositive (9,068 males and 997 females) giving seropositivity rate of 14.7 per 100 in Manipur against all India figure of 2.6. It should be noted that Manipur with only 0.2% of India's population contributes nearly 8% of India's total HIV positive cases. Reported AIDS cases in the state are 650 and reported AIDS related deaths are 137.

The detailed breakup of HIV prevalence in Manipur is given in Tables 1, 2a and 2b.

One of the major reasons for injecting drug use is easy availability of drugs. Other factors include social, economic and other related issues. A study in Churachandpur among IDUs (Sarkar et al. 1991) revealed that heroin was used by all IDUs a majority of

Table 1. Epidemiological Analysis of HIV/AIDS In Manipur

1. Period: September, 1986 to May, 2000

2. Number of blood samples:	Sero-surveillance	Sentinel Surveillance	Total
Screened	47,618	20,830	68,448
3. Number of Positives	7431	2,634	10,065
4. Number of females	997	—	997
5. Number of AIDS cases	650	—	650
6. Number of deaths	137	—	137
7. Sero-positivity Rate per 1000 samples screened	156.05	126.45	147.05

8. Sero-positivity among different High-Risk Groups under surveillance

8.1. Sero-surveillance

Risk Groups	*Number Screened*	*Number Positive*	*Sero-positivity rate*
Heterosexually Promiscuous	5885	336	5.71
Homosexuals	15	—	—
Injecting Drug Users (IDUs)	8705	5062	58.15
Blood Donors	10,587	218	2.05
Blood Recipients	998	47	4.71
Antenatal Mothers	2658	63	2.37
Patient on Dialysis	—	—	—
Suspected ARC/ AIDS Patients	1524	213	13.98
Relatives of AIDS Patients	250	85	34.00
Others	16,996	1,407	8.28
Sub-total	47,618	7431	15.61

Courtesy: MACS

Table 2a. Age-Sex Proportion of HIV Positive Cases (Sero-surveillance)

Age-Group	*Males*	*Females*	*Total*	*% of total Positives*
0–10 Years	82	69	151	2.03
11–20 Years	743	91	834	11.23
21–30 Years	3997	550	4547	61.25
31–40 Years	1371	221	1592	21.44
41 & Above	235	65	300	4.04
Total	6428	976	7424	100.00
Unknown	—	—	7	—
Total	6428	976	7431	—

Table 2b. District-wise Distribution of HIV Positive Cases (Sero-surveillance)

District	*Number of Samples Screened*	*Number of HIV Positives*	*Sero-positivity rate (%)*	*District Percentage*
Imphal	27814	4858	17.47	68.69
Thoubal	3622	610	16.84	8.63
Bishnupur	1964	342	17.41	4.84
Churachandpur	1526	489	32.04	6.91
Ukhrul	651	253	38.86	3.58
Senapati	904	243	26.88	3.44
Tamenglong	204	13	6.37	0.18
Chandel	1007	264	26.23	3.73
Total	37692	7072		100
Unknown	9926	359		
Total	47618	7431		

Courtesy: MACS

whom were males between the ages of 15 and 35 years. The education levels of these youths were quite high, 78.5% having studied upto high school or pre-university levels. Unemployment accounted for 53 percent of the IDUs, out of which 34 percent were students. Earlier estimates stated that female injecting drug users constituted 5–8% (Sarkar, 1993). Recent report indicates an increase to 10 percent (Sharma, 1999). The overall dropout rates from schools are very high.

In Manipur the most important mode of transmission of HIV has been the sharing of injection equipment during injecting drug use, which in turn has been made possible due to the ease of supply and availability of heroin in the region. Table 3 gives the quality of drug seized since 1987. This demonstrates continued drug trafficking in

Table 3. Comparative Crime Figures in Manipur under NDPS Act
(with effect from 1987 till date)

Year	No. of Cases	No. of Persons Arrested	Heroin Seized	Ganja Seized	Opium Seized
1987	338	549	5 kg 376 gm	488.6 gm	28 gm
1988	370	424	4 kg 945 gm	554 kg	2 gm 814 mg
1989	389	507	10 kg 226 gm	7076 kg	384 gm 130 mg
1990	412	540	1.72 kg 905 mg	10425 kg 628 mg	62 gm
1991	406	478	1.635 kg 780 mg	5268 kg 443 gm	57 gm
1992	629	710	9.633 kg 157 mg	7087 kg 252 gm	35 gm 16 mg
1993	421	469	3.995 kg 133 mg	32676 kg 635 mg	—
1994	418	542	5.903 gm 933 mg	21140 kg 865 gm	1gm
1995	92	116	467 gm 900 mg	4239 kg 770 gm	—
1996	117	145	1.494 gm 630 mg	1043 kg 319 gm	19 gm
1997	168	222	3.338 gm 985 mg	16767 kg 10 gm	—
1998	127	164	7 kg 269 gm 588 mg	3660 kg 541 gm	1 kg 450 gm

Taken from the publication entitiled "A situational analysis of the HIV/AIDS epidemic and responses in the state of Manipur"—a report prepared for the Australian Agency for international development.

the region and the significant amount of heroin, ganja and opium seized every year. The agencies responsible for drug enforcement are the Border Security Force, Excise, Central Excise and Custom Departments, Narcotic Control Bureau, Police Department and the Department of Border Affairs and Narcotics. While enforcement agencies continue in their attempts to curb drug trafficking, it was clear from interviews that this alone was not sufficient to stem the flow of drugs into the region. The active help and participation of the community in addressing this problem is essential.

In the beginning most of the Heroin Drug Abuse was observed along the National Highway No. 39, which originates from Moreh to India-Myanmar Border and runs towards Dimapur in Nagaland. But now, this characteristic has been lost and there is hardly any village which is not affected.

In Manipur, the addicts start using the drug orally either by smoking or inhaling (chasing the dragon). Then they switch on to injecting (fixing) often sharing with friends/peers or lovers. While injecting they share the injecting equipment like needles and syringes or improvised syringes like plastic ink-dropper fitted with needle among a group of 2 or 3 normally but sometimes as many as seven at one go. They often use plastic phials/droppers in place of syringes to evade arrest by the police. Many use drugs daily.

There is great frustration among students due to frequent bandhs (strikes) and other disruptions. The insurgency movement also contributes to unrest and instability, forcing educational and other institutions to function sub-optimally. This have got adverse effect among the youths. Only information and education alone has succeeded in arresting the problem. There is need to rectify the dissatisfaction of youths and to improve the deteriorating academic atmosphere in the state. Manipur is economically in a bad shape without much development in the private and social sector. Political unrest and ethnic problems have added to the existing woes in the state. All these fundamental issues need addressing in containing the menace of drug abuse and AIDS.

Some of the findings with regard to drug abuse in Manipur are:

1. Next to Heroin, other drugs used are: Opium, alcohol, morphine, dextropropoxyphene, nitrazepam, pentazocine, diazepam, amphetamine, phensedyle, buprenorphine, fortwin and codeine.
2. The reasons for using drugs were pleasure (58.0%), curiosity (50.2%), per pressure (25.7%). The main sources of money for buying drugs were from the family (80.9%), personal income (48.6%), through selling drugs (25%), borrowing (39.2%), stealing (32.1%). On the average, a drug addict spents Rs. 87 per day (Rs. 2301 per month) only on drugs. 88% were unemployed or self-employed.
3. Many of the IDUs did not clean their injecting equipment (42.6%), whereas 50.2 % clean only with plain water and 6.6% boiled it.
4. 90.5% of the IDUs were between the age group 15–35 years and 9.2% were between 35–44 years of age. Females constituted about 3.6% of the drug addicts.
5. Among the IDUs, 68.3% were unmarried, 29.3% were married and 2.4% were divorced or widowed.
6. Majority of the IDUs had prison experiences, had made several attempts to get rid of drugs. The relapse rate was more than 80%.
7. 40% of the IDUs had sexual partners 14.9% used to go to commercial sex workers.
8. There is emergence of new case of 15.6% (0–12 months), 14.4% (12–24 months), 70% & above (24 months & more) (Report collected from some NGOs.).

9. The sero prevalence rate of HIV among IDUs has increased to 55.7% during 1994, 54% during 1995, 64% during 1996, 76.9% during 1997, 67.6% & 72.7% during 1998, 55.5% during 1999.
10. The HIV infection is still spreading among the IDUs population and through them to their sexual partners and their offsprings.
11. Among the N.E. states, Manipur, Nagaland are badly affected followed by Mizoram. The correct picture of other states is not clear in absence of sufficient data.
12. The drug trafficking from Golden Triangle through Myanmar is a major problem of Mizoram, Manipur, Nagaland, District east of Brahmaputra in Arunachal Pradesh. This problem is further compounded by hilly terrain and poor communication network in the region.
13. There is no adequate NGOs network in other states except in Manipur and Mizoram, in the drug abuse prevention area. There is also shortage of trained personnel in counselling work and implementation of drug deaddiction centres and rehabilitation.
14. There is pilot projects in Thoubal, Churanchandpur. The findings may provide baseline data. There are approximately 20 NGOs of which 12 NGOs are running with 15–30 bed each.
15. The drug abuse picture in the N.E. is grim and calls for immediate action.

Action taken by Manipur Government on drug demand reduction: (with assistance from Govt. of India).

1. 130 bedded Drug Deaddiction Centre has started functioning at Imphal since January, 1992.
2. Drug Deaddiction Centres constructed at Imphal, Churachandpur, Chandel and Moreh.
3. 95 doctors trained in drug deaddiction during 1993–95.
4. One pilot project on community based drug deaddiction started at Impahl, Churachandpur and Thoubal in collaboration with the All India Institute of Medical Sciences, New Delhi.
5. State Govt. is working in close collaboration with NGOs in the field of drug deaddiction. Various activities are being carried out i.e. IEC, training courses, workshops. Manipur State has got well established Manipur State AIDS Control Programme which looks after the HIV/AIDS control activities in collaboration with National AIDS control organisation (NACO).

The Technical Resource Group on Intravenous Drug Users and AIDS has been constituted by NACO, with the Director, RIMS as Chairman of the TRG on the 31st March, 1998. The Group has recommended various best practices in the prevention and control of HIV/AIDS among intravenous drug users.

The various practices prevalent in the country are:

1. Home Detoxification.
2. Detoxification Camp.
3. Detoxification and Rehabilitation Centres.
4. Intervention and Care projects:
   a) Needle syringe Exchange Programme,
   b) Bleach and Teach Programme,
   c) Keeping own Syringe,
   d) Drop in Centres,
   e) Substitution Therapy.
5. Condom Promotion.

The main goal was (i) to reduce the HIV seroprevalence rate among IDUs by 10% in high endemic areas and by 20% in low endemic areas by targetted intervention and care. (ii) to prevent/minimise spread of HIV to the spouse/sexual partners of IDUs. (iii) to prevent/minimise spread of HIV amongst IDUs.

The components of the intervention programmes are:

1. Needle syringe exchange programme.
2. Bleach and Teach programme.
3. Substitution Therapy.
4. Condom Promotion.
5. Establishment of Drop in Centres as the service Centres of the above components.
6. Education and counselling.
7. Encouragement of voluntary HIV Ab. testing.
8. Organisation of self groups like Narcotic Anomymous.
9. Organisation of care services, like home care, continuum of care and dedicated treatment centres like "Hospic".

The Manipur State AIDS Control Society has launched an intervention and care programme (RIAC). This may be consulted by the other societies in formulating their own programme.

The TRG strongly recommends the Intervention programme for harm minimisation of IDUs & AIDS. It also recommends to the states to formulate suitable AIDS Policy and Drug Abuse Policy.

Suggestions for prevention of drug abuse/drug demand reductions are:

1. To ensure availability and accessibility of minimum drug deaddiction, detoxification, treatment and rehabilitation services as part of the comprehensive primary health care services.
2. To create mass awakening among the people particularly the young people about the harmful effects of drugs and its social, economic and developmental consequences through organisation of intensive and extensive health promotion/education campaigns involving the community.
3. To establish training centres for training doctors, nurses, paramedics, counsellors, social workers, community leaders, volunteers etc. on drug demand reduction.
4. To create 'Resource Centre' for imparting skills.
5. To promote and support community participation.
6. To ensure physical, social and economic rehabilitation of the drug users so that they may become useful members of the society.
7. To check drug trafficking by strengthening N.D. & P.S. Act, 1985.
8. To strengthen existing system of counselling.
9. Use of peer network for IEC.
10. Programme to increase condom use.
11. Programme targetted to youth awareness.
12. Expansion of voluntary confidential testing and encouragement of premarital testing.
13. Monitoring and evaluation with indicators.

REFERENCES

Situations analysis of HIV and drug abuse in the north-eastern region of India, published by Regional Medical Research Centre, N.E. Region (ICMR) 1998.

Draft document on Intravenous Drug Users and AIDS (A status report prepared by the Technical Resource Group on Intravenous Drug users and AIDS), Dec., 1999.

A situational analysis of the HIV/AIDS epidemic and responses in the state of Manipur—A report prepared for the Australian Agency for International Development.

CARC Calling, Bulletin of the Centre for AIDS Research and Control, Vol. 3, No. 3, July–Sept. 1990. ICMR, Page 2–6.

Report of DDA Programme in Manipur presented by Health Department during the Regional Review Meeting of N.E. States on 2–4 April, 1998.

Sarkar et al., 1993. Rapid spread of HIV in injecting drug users in North East India—Bulletin of Narcotics, Vol. 45. pp. 95–103.

Sharma. U., Unpublished data, 1999.

"Epidemiological analysis of HIV/AIDS in Manipur", published by the Manipur State AIDS Control Society, May, 2000.

The Role of Churches in Containing the Ethnic Conflicts in Manipur

Lal Dena

The objective of this paper is to give an evaluation of the role of the All Manipur Christian Organisation (AMCO) towards the resolution of the Kuki-Naga conflict between 1992–1994 and then offer a critical enquiry into the roots of this violent conflict.

Deeply aware of the need for a single organisation encompassing all the churches in Manipur and the urgency of its affiliation to other national Christian organisations in view of the newly emerging critical issues. Some prominent Church leaders met at the Manipur Baptist Convention (MBC) Conference Hall on 28 February, 1989 at 11 AM with Rev. Douzapao Haokip and Rev. W. Roel as Chairman and Secretary respectively and formed the All Manipur Christian Action Committee (AMCAC). As there had been many suggestions from different quarters, the newly formed AMCAC was changed into the All Manipur Christian Organisation on 4 July, 1989, having its correspondence office at the SDA Mission at Chingmeirong, Imphal, which was later on registered under the Society Act of 1860. Among others, the main objectives of the AMCO are as given below:

a) to protect the member churches from social injustices, false allegations and accusations, illegal practices, attacks and counter-attacks from within and without;
b) to create healthy environment conducive to mutual understanding and cooperation among the Christian community irrespective of race, caste or creed;

c) to fight against communalism in order to bring about harmonious and peaceful co-existence and brotherly neighbourhood;
d) to fight against corruption of any kind and at any level in society and to help the government suppress illegal trafficking in drugs and contraband items;
e) to set up a common platform for redressal of the grievances of Christians and act as a liaison between the people and the government as good citizens;
f) to encourage the existing Church bodies and para-Church bodies to do and extend mutual help to one another for the promotion of better Christian understanding and co-operation;
g) to safeguard the freedom of the Christian Churches, para-church institutions and preaching of the gospel and to infuse mutual respect among church leaders and secular leaders or any authority;
h) to safeguard and protect the properties of the Christian churches, moveable and unmoveable from illegal requisition and demolition; and
i) to coordinate relief measures of any kind in order to assist victims of natural calamities and accidents in consultation and collaboration with other Christian agencies and government machineries.

The first challenge of the AMCO was the outbreak of the Kuki-Naga conflict from June, 1992 which continued till 1994. Soon, the AMCO began to involve itself by convening its emergency meeting on 25 September, 1992 at the MBC Conference Hall, Imphal and made the following appeals to the warring factions in the conflict:

1. All past wrongs of the communities concerned should be forgotten and forgiven in the name of Christ, their common Lord and Saviour.
2. The Christian members in Manipur in general and the Christians in Imphal area in particular were requested to observe social harmony, and genuine Christian fellowship among them by not yielding to false rumours.
3. All Christians were requested to refrain from all kinds of political and social conflicts which might bring tension and discord in their fellowship and relationship.
4. The government be requested to investigate the root cause of all these troubles and disturbances and to bring about justice and peace among the people of the state.

Along with this appeal, the AMCO also set up a peace mission consisting of prominent Church leaders to visit all the affected places and districts. In spite of the best efforts of the AMCO, the situation did not improve but instead became from bad to worse because of the burning of houses and massacres. The AMCO again made a ferrent appeal particularly to the underground brothers to once again a serious rethinking on the futality of violence and on the following points: to stop killing and torturing innocent civilians and extorting money; to stop burning houses and villages; to resolve problem by peaceful means through dialogue based on justice and truth; to reflect on the fact that they were all the children of the same God; and to create a fear and tension free atmosphere so that displaced persons could go back to their respective villages in peace.

At the same time, the AMCO approached both the state and central governments, North East India Christian Organisation for Relief and Development, Catholic Relief Society and even UN Agencies like World Food Programme for more relief and rehabilitation funds for the victims of the communal clash. On 28 September, 1993, the Goodwill Mission from the Council of Baptist Churches in North East India (CBCNEI), Guwahati met the leaders of the United Naga Council (UNC) and the Kuki Inpi, Manipur (KIM) including the members of the AMCO peace mission for immediate restoration of normalcy and unconditional ceasefire on 2 October, 1993. Also, the emergency joint meeting of UNC, KIM and the AMCO peace mission the next day with John Joseph, National Minorities Commission, Government of India, at the Bishop's House, Mantripukhri, Imphal, decided to apprise of the Prime Minister, on 30 September, 1993 by highlighting the following points: (1) alleged failure of the state machinery to maintain peace and order in the state; (2) case of launching the "Operation October," utmost care must be taken not to cause unwarranted harassment and suffering to the innocent masses; (3) adoption of non-partesan and neutral attitude free from political vendetta; (4) immediate release of adequate compensation to the victims of the conflict for loss of lives and properties and rehabilitation of displaced persons; (5) provision of adequate protection to all cultivators in all vulnerable villages for peaceful harvest; and, (6) creation of lasting peace in the state. Further, with the initiative of John Joseph, the Kuki and the Naga leadership met separately and then jointly agreed with him in the presence of the Chief Minister and the Governor of the State on the following points:

1. There should be a "Peace Period" for three months.
2. To enable the members to contact the contending parties, a two weeks time should be given.
3. The modus operandi for going about to contact the concerned persons should be worked out separately.
4. The government was to give all help and assistance such as vehicles, and finance as and when required.
5. Security forces and police personnels must maintain absolute impartiality in dealing with the Kukis and Nagas.
6. No Kuki or Naga armed forces and policemen be deployed in the affected areas.
7. Substantial ex-gratia and compensation should be given to the grieved families by the government immediately.
8. The public roads and highways, both the national and the state, should be effectively made free and the safety of passengers be ensured by the state government.
9. Return of displaced persons to their original places be ensured by the government to enable them to harvest their fields during the "Peace Period".

In this way, though incapacitated by many limitations, the AMCO left no stone unturned to implement the points of agreements in letter and spirit. With relief aids in cash or in kind, the AMCO also visited all the refugee camps in the hill districts and consoled the injured in hospitals with gifts and prayers during the whole period of the conflict.

The National Council of Churches in India (NCCI) in cooperation with the North East India Christian Council (NEICC) also visited Manipur three times to help resolve the conflict. Aware of the ineffectiveness of appeals, pamphlets and peace-rallies, the AMCO leadership decided to change its approach which might booster their courage to face the real crux of the conflict. Thus in its meeting with the representatives from the NCCI on 3 April, 1994 at Hotel Ashoka, Imphal, it reiterated the need to seek ways and means to meet the underground brethrens of the Nagas and Kukis.

Critical Appraisal of the Conflict

It may be pointed out that the two communities involved in the conflict are almost cent per cent Christians. Of them, majority of them are Baptist Christians. Despite their claims of being Christians and their preaching about the love of god, they are the ones who committed such inhuman atrocities and massacres on their fellow-human beings. Could this be taken as the failure of Christianity in the hill areas of Manipur? It appears that a Kuki is first a Kuki and then a Christian; and a Naga becomes a Naga first and then a Christian. In other words, their loyalty to Christ is subordinated to their loyalty to their ethnic community. But a true and committed Christian is a Christian first and all others are secondary. This is to say that it is not Christianity which fails but the so-called Christians who fail to live upto the standard of biblical teachings.

Impact of Environmental Upheavals in Manipur

B. Manihar Sharma

Introduction

Due to the close interactions among the various organisms and the surrounding environments, a net-work of natural systems exists on the earth. This system is termed as *Ecosystem* and the various ecosystems of the world form a unified system known as the *Biosphere*. In the International Conference on Human Environment held in Stockholm in 1977 stressed that the environment is to be viewed as *total* environment which comprises three types of environment viz. (i) physical environment (abiotic and climatic state variables such as air, soil and water), (ii) biological environment (biotic state variables i.e. plants, animals and micro-organisms), and (iii) socio-cultural environment (cultural heritage, social and ethnic customs, beliefs etc.). It is noteworthy that each and every part of each environment component is highly responsible for the functioning and regulation of an ecosystem. Any perturbation in the components which are superimposed on one another would result to the degradation of the Ecological Balance (Homeostasis) of the ecosystem. Degradations in the physical and biological environments (popularly termed as environment) in the various land and aquatic habitats often cause serious ecological and socio-economic turmoils.

Environmental Issues in Manipur

Various environmental degradations have occurred in the state in the past two decades that had caused much damages and disturbances to the people and the habitats. In the present paper some of the environmental problems with long term effects are highlighted briefly. The impacts of the degradation of forests, wetland systems as well as mismanagement of the other environmental attributes are presented herewith with the hope that the same may be able to throw some light towards planning the ways and means to protect and rectify the same at the earliest.

Forest Status: Its Impacts

The total area of the forests in Manipur has been reported to be 15, 154 sq km constituting 67.7% of the geographical area. According to the Forest Survey of India (FSI) the area rose to a peak value of 17,679 sq km (79.2%) in 1990 but the area of total forests decreased from 17,558 sq km in 1995 to 17,418 sq km by 1997. According to these reports only an area of 4,937 sq km that constitutes 22.11% of geographical area represent the 'dense' or 'true' forests while the remaining areas are designated as 'scrub' or grassland dominated areas which in the true sense can hardly be regarded as forests. According to the reports of the National Remote Sensing Agency (NRSA) based on satellite imagery, the area of dense (*true*) forest decreased from 10,995 sq km (49.1%) in 1988–89 to only 719.3 sq km (3.2%) in 1990s. It cannot in the present context be denied that *almost* all the forests in the state have been degraded to a great extent thereby reducing the forest areas to *scrubs* (grasslands with a few poles of trees scattered hither and thither). According to the Forest Survey of India, the various reasons for the fast removal of the forests in the state are 'burning' of the forests (99%) due to *shifting* cultivation (*Jhumming* practice) and hunting of animals whereas felling of trees by the local people for fuelwood hardly constitute 1% of forest removal in the state.

The state is one of the regions having vast areas of forests under shifting cultivation in India as about 83,526 families are reportedly practising it. The total area under jhum cultivation had been 1,832 sq km in 1976, which gradually increased to 3,600 sq km in 1983 and 4,905 sq km by 1990 according to reports of FSI and NRSA. The largest area cleared for jhumming in the state is found in Senapati district (28.3%) which is successively followed by the areas in Churachandpur, Ukhrul, Tamenglong and Chandel districts (Table 1). The serious environmental effects of forest removal through

Table 1. Present Status of the Forests in Manipur

	Parameter		Source
1. Area of Forests in sq km (1997)			
(i) Dense forests	4,937	(22.1%)	Forest Department, Manipur (1999)
(ii) Open (scrub) forests	12, 481	(55.9%)	
(iii) Total forests	17,418	(78%)	
2. Area of dense forests in sq km	719.3	(3.2%)	NRSA (1990)
3. Forest area under Jhum cultivation in sq km			NRSA (1990)
Senapati District	1,388	(28.3%)	
Churachandpur	1,232	(25.1%)	
Ukhrul	718	(14.6%)	
Tamenglong	675	(14.0%)	
Chandel	655	(13.3%)	
Imphal	168.8	(3.4%)	
Thoubal	51.1	(1.0%)	
Bishnupur	17.3	(0.3%)	
Total	4,905.2		
4. Annual Afforestation: Deforestation ratio	1: 18.3		Sharma (1997)
5. Forest Loss Index of the state	0.04		Sharma (1997)
6. Annual fuel wood production in cu m (1997)	29,078		Forest Dept., Manipur (1998)
7. Annual reduction in fuel wood production in cu m during 1990–1995	11,300		Sharma (1997)
8. Threatened plant species			Sharma (1997)
Trees: Phoebe hainesiana, Juglans regia, Rhus hookeri, Grewia elastica, Flacourtia cataphracta, Butea frondosa, Aphanomixis polystachys, Magnolia griffithii, Cycas pectinata, Podocarpus wallichii.			
Orchids: Cymbidium giganteum, Arundina graminifolia, Ascocentrum ampelleceum, Dendrobium arachnites, Dendrobium densiflorum, Dendrobium nobile, Kalimpongea narajitii, Paphiopedilum insigne, Paphiopedilum villosum, Spiranthes sp., Vanda coerulea			
Aromatic and medicinal plants: Aquilaria agallocha, Dioscorea deltoidea, Rauwolffia serpentina.			

burning are the occurrence of a number of ecological catastrophes viz., flash floods, soil and land degradation, loss of fertile top soil and health hazards. Due to heavy burning of forests in almost all the hills in the various districts by the end of winter and onset of spring (February to May) enormous liberation of smokes has become a usual phenomenon. The direct effects are the occurrences of respiratory diseases like *bronchitis*, *asthma* and *goitre* to the hill people especially the children and youths. An immediate environmentally safe cultivation practice like *Terrace* cultivation and modified jhum without the burning phase may be implemented. Due to reckless burning of the forests the important tree species like pine, teak, *Phoebe* sp., *Juglans* sp., *Castanopsis* sp. *Quercus* species have depleted leading to the status of threatened species. Besides, a number of plants (over 65 species) comprising shrubs, bamboos, canes, orchids, aromatic and medicinal plants some of which are endemic (strictly local) are threatened at different levels (Sharma 1997).

Some other detrimental consequences of the heavy deforestation in the state need to be emphasized. As the rate of afforestation is much less as compared to the deforestation rate, the annual afforestation: deforestation ratio is found to be 1: 18.3 (Sharma 1997) and this ratio far exceeds the ratios for India and the world i.e. 1: 14 and 1: 10 respectively (Newman 1990). When compared to the 'forest loss indices' of the countries of the world (Thomas et al. 1996), Manipur and other states of the North East have High forest indices above 0.04 and hence these forests are designated as areas of 'critical concern' (Sharma 1997). Since 1986 where 70,264 cu m of fuel-wood was produced, a gradual decreasing trend in fuelwood production has been noticed excepting some rises in 1995–96. The fuelwood production has been noticed excepting some rise in 1995–96. The fuelwood production stands at 29,078 cu m by 1997 (Forest Department, Manipur 1998).

In the light of the facts already mentioned it is hightime to work out the remedial measures to save the forests of the state and protect the environment from further deterioration. In this regard, environmental awareness camps should be arranged so that people should resort to the eco-friendly alternatives to jhum cultivation. It is essential to mobilise the public mass to take up afforestation programmes in association with concerned organisations and departments of the government.

Wetland Ecosystems

The 'Wetlands' are defined as very shallow aquatic areas (less than 6 metres in depth) which are subjected to a number of physico-chemical stresses. The International Union for Conservation of Nature and Natural Resources has viewed the wetlands as shallow aquatic bodies which are on the verge of extinction unless immediate measures are taken up to protect them (Ramsar Convention Bureau 1997). According to the environmentalists the wetland has the capability of carrying out specific vital functions like flood control, water storage, groundwater recharge, sediment retention, nutrient accumulation and stabilisation of the local climatic conditions.

Most of the waterbodies of Manipur like the aged lakes and ponds are subjected to numerous environmental threats like artificial eutrophication and encroachments. It may be pointed out that most of our lakes have reached the status of wetlands. There were reportedly about 500 lakes in the valley of the state by the beginning of the 20th century. Hardly 55 lakes were found existing in the state by 1950s. Besides the Loktak lake most important lake in the North East and a Ramsar site, some lakes like Ikop, Waithou, Ngakrapat and Loushipat are found to be the important lakes existing now in the state. These lakes are much threatened due to artificial eutrophication and human encroachments for cultivation and fish farming. Highly degraded lakes in the state are Kharungpat, Pumlen, Loukoipat, Utrapat, Sanapat, Yaralpat and Poiroupat. Almost all the lakes and ponds are subjected to a number of environmental threats. Some of the major causes for polluting water and degrading the lakes are (i) disposal of domestic garbages, (ii) leaching of chemical fertilisers due to agricultural and piscicultural activities, (iii) encroachments for paddy cultivation, (iv) draining of insecticides, pesticides and weedicides from the neighbouring crop fields to rainfall and (v) misuse of the toxic chemicals for catching fishes.

The morphometric analyses, physico-chemical properties of water and ecological studies of the macrophytes of Loktak lake were undertaken by Devi, N.B. (1993) while studies in Waithou lake and Utrapat lake were carried out by Devi, O.I. (1993) and Devi, K.I. (1998) respectively. The important characteristic features of these lakes have been summarised in Table 2. Some of the major environmental and ecological changes that have taken place in these life supporting lakes are highlighted in this table.

Table 2. Morphometry and Ecological Features of the important Lakes in Manipur

Parameters	*Loktak*	*Waithou*	*Utrapat*
Altitude (m)	768	785	783
Maximum length (km)	20.5	1.04	0.74
Maximum breadth (km)	8.8	0.94	0.65
Surface area (sq km)	180.4	0.99	0.37
Maximum depth (m)	5.2	1.7	2.2
Minimum depth (m)	0.9	0.7	0.7
Mean depth (m)	3.0	1.2	1.4
Mean depth/max. depth ratio	0.58	0.72	0.63
Shoreline (km)	55.8	3.49	2.47
Shoreline development	1.17	0.98	1.15
Development of volume	1.76	2.17	1.85
Basin shape	saucer	saucer	saucer
Basin slope	gentle	gentle	gentle
Bottom texture	silted	silted	silted
Average annual rainfall (cm)	212.9	130.5	180.3
Average maximum temp. (°c)	31.2	33.1	30.5
Average minimum temp. (°c)	5.3	2.8	4.1
Mean volume (cu km)	0.55	0.001	0.001
Surface area/volume ratio	328.0	826.6	703.8
Total catchment area (sq km)	962.0	326.2	250.3
pH value	6.0–9.3	7.4–8.3	6.2–9.8
Dissolved carbondioxide (ppm)	1.0–39.3	1.0–35.0	4.0–75.0
Dissolved oxygen (ppm)	0.4–9.5	2.2–7.4	1.0–9.0
Plant biomass (g/m^2)	230–900	423–1,306	138–581
Plant production (g/m^2/yr)	181–1,241	1,350–1,601	339–410
Trophic status	Eutrophic	Eutrophic	Eutrophic
Environmental threats: causes	(i) Human encroachment (ii) Water inundation due to Ithai barrage (iii) Misuse of pesticides etc. (iv) Overaccumulation of organic debris (v) Poaching of wild life (vi) water quality much deteriorated	(i) Encroachment (ii) Misuse of chemicals (iii) water quality poor	(i) Encroachment (ii) Misuse of chemicals (iii) water quality poor

Loktak Lake

Situated in the Bishenpur district, the Loktak lake represents the largest freshwater lake in the North East. The Keibul Lamjao which is the only native home of the endangered brow-antlered deer *Sangai* (*Cervus eldi eldi*) represents a unique vast expanse of floating mats (*phumdi*) located inside the lake. The unique up and down movement of these floating mats in the different seasons has now been disturbed due to inundation of water caused by the Ithai barrage. The consequence is the disturbance to the very existence, breeding and adaptive natures of the Sangai and other endemic wild species. The existence of a number of economic plants like *Saccharum* sp., *Setaria pumila*, *Alpinia nigra*, *Hedychium spicatum* etc. has also been much disturbed. Though all the possible steps have been taken up to protect the Sangai and other wild life species in the Keibul Lamjao National Park, illegal and intermittent killings have threatened the existence of the precious Sangai and other animals including a number of bird species. Altogether 138 species of plants representing 88 genera are found distributed in the phumdi and non-phumdi (clear water) zones of the lake. The growth and productivity of *Trapa natans* (*Heikak*) in the lake has been much disturbed thereby decreasing the production of the fruit which is an important staple substitute for rice. The production of the edible fruit and rhizome (*thamchet* and *thambou*) of lotus (*Nelumbo nucifera*) as well as edible underground rhizome of *Nymphaea stellata* (*Lemphu*) have also decreased. Due to a number of environmntal perturbations, the occurrence of the rare wild rice *Oryza rufipogon* (*wainu chara*) and the rare ornamental orchid *Spiranthes sinensis* have been greatly disturbed. Due to the disturbence of the breeding grounds of the important fish varieties like *Anabas* sp. *Colisa fasciatus*, *Colisa chuna*, *Punctius ticto* and *Esomus danricus*, the production of these species have been found decreasing significantly. With the gradual increase in the level of pollution of water along with significant decrease in dissolved oxygen contents the precious *Channa orientalis*, *Channa Punctatus* and *Channa striatus* can no longer thrive and hence these species are on the decline. A perusal of the several physico-chemical and ecological characters of the lake (Table 2) clearly indicate the enhanced *eutrophication* (nutrient enrichment causing pollution) going on inside the lake environment that threatens the life and the very existence of this precious lake.

The overall condition of the lake as well as the socio-economic status of over 60,000 farmers and fishermen including those in over 600 families in floating huts have seriously been affected since the construction of Ithai barrage and commissioning of the Loktak Hydro Electric Project in 1983–84. On the average over 30,000 hectares of paddy field are usually submerged annually due to inundated water. The planners have still to realise the agony of the Ithai barrage affected people and should resort to the viable ways and means to solve the problems to the possible extent.

Besides the occurrence of water pollution and eutrophication intermittently in the various regions of the lake (now a Ramsar site) since 1990, more serious degradation in the water quality of the lake has occurred since July, 2000. In the various areas of the lake in Thanga, Moirang and Sendra especially at Nongmaikhong, Manungpat, Leingangpat, Kharungpat, Lamyai, Phamlok, Ngakrapat, Ikop and many other places, the water quality had deteriorated to a great extent (turning the water to brownish-yellow colour with pungent smell, very low dissolved oxygen content etc.). The people have suffered from a number of skin diseases, fever and respiratory troubles. This has also caused the death of large populations of fish species (especially *Colisa* species, *Punctius* sp., *Esomus* sp. etc.) as well as a number of water fowl species. This may be attributed to a number of factors such as (i) Vast accumulation of plant debris that starts rotting and decomposing on the water surface as well as on the bottom sediment. This is mainly caused by leaving the excised parts of *Euryale ferox*, *Trapa*, *Hydrilla*, *Ceratophyllum* etc. after harvesting on the water surface, (ii) Use of insecticides in the water for catching fishes, (iii) Use of excessive amount of fertilizers, pesticides and other chemicals in the paddy fields in and around the water bodies, (iv) Non-removal of the thick mats of weeds, *Lemnna*, *Salvinia* etc. Monitoring of the water quality by all concerned (government as well as public organisations) and taking up immediate steps and means to rectify the same by the concerned authorities is called for before serious catastrophes arise. Removal of the organic debris that floats on the water surface as well as those accumulated at the bottom of the lake is to be carried out as an immediate measure. Revitalisation of water through manual as well as mechanical means would also be much helpful.

Waithou Lake

This oval shaped lake is situated at Waithou at a distance of 17 km due south of Imphal. The morphometric as well as ecological survey indicate the advanced eutrophication going on in the lake. Encroachments for cultivation and fish farming are the potent factors for the degradation of the lake. Only 35 macrophytic plant species are found distributed in the different seasons of the year. Production of the economic plants like Trapa, Euryale ferox, Nelumbo, Nymphea species have gone down to a great extent. Physico-chemical analysis of the lake water also revealed much deteriorartion in the water quality. The lake had been the favourable habitat of the delicious fish *Labeo bata* (Ngaton). With the deterioration of the lake following the construction of the Chekshabi barrage and ring bund in 1970s, the fish species has completely vanished from the lake.

Utrapat Lake

This lake located at Nambol due 20 km south of Imphal is in the advanced stage of eutrophication. The existence of the lake is much threatened due to human enroachments and interferences. At present only about 26 macrophytic plant species are found distributed in the different seasons of the year. The water quality has been found much degraded as revealed by the physico-chemical analyses. This is much responsible for the significant decrease in the production of the economic plants like *Trapa*, *Nymphoides*, *Nymphea*, *Nelumbo* species etc.

The Sanapat located at Nambol is a small lake having 1.97 sq km in area and it supports only about 32 plant species. The production of the economic plants has been found much decreased. The water quality, habitat as well as the morphological characters of the lake has been degraded due to human encroachments through cultivation and pisciculture. The Ikop lake having an area of 6.2 sq km is situated in Thoubal at a distance of about 40 km due south-east of Imphal. The lake threatened due to artificial eutrophication through human encroachment has exhibited the occurrence of only 26 macrophytic plant species. As water quality is much degraded the production of the economic plants has significantly decreased. Similar is the fate of the dying lakes like Yaralpat, Poiroupat, Kharungpat, Pumlen, Khoidumpat.

It is worthwhile to mention herewith that unless the environmental and conservational measures are taken up immediately, the degradations in the lakes mentioned above may progress rapidly which would ultimately lead to the death of these lakes.

Other Environmental Strategies: Some of the environmental mismanagements which require appropriate attention are mentioned briefly as follows:

1. The smokes from the burning of coal in many brick fields of Manipur are directly liberated into the atmosphere without any form of treatment. This has caused damage to the crops, vegetables and has contaminated the water in ponds and lakes. Respiratory problems have been caused to the young kids in the vicinity of these areas. Appropriate treatment devices such as use of electrostatic precipitators may be suggested.
2. There is huge liberations of carbon shoots and smokes through the burning of kerosene in lamps with large wicks (*podon* in Manipuri). This has been a usual daily practice in hundreds of women markets in the capital, as well as numerous villages in the state. Electrification in such markets would be highly necessary.
3. Misuse and overuse of chemicals like Thionel-Endosulphan, Pestoban, Rogo-300 and similar poisonous chemicals have been used in the fields as well as in the ponds, lakes and streams as a means of catching fishes without strains. Such malpractices cause dreaded diseases like UDS in the fishes. We may recall the serious outbreak of this epidemic in fishes throughout the state in 1992 that took the lives of a few people rendering hundreds of people hospitalised.
4. Stray disposal of wastes such as organic debris from vegetable markets, domestic kitchens and piling them up in the markets and road corners has been the most regular routine practice in the whole state. After levelling these raw wastes temporary huts are constructed and people have started inhabiting in such areas. It is highly undesirable as methane and carbonmonoxide gases (which are lethal) may accumulate and disrupt after the lapse of many years. We may recall the instant death of 5 tribal brothers in Churachandpur in 1999 due to the liberation of carbon-monoxide in an earthern well. The immediate suggestion is to throw these garbages in a garbage pit which after filling

up may be subjected to composting or burning of the garbages in the pit after separating the plastic, polythene and PVC wastes.

5. The population pressure indices of Imphal (15.55), Thoubal (14.12) and Bishnupur (9.80) are comparatively higher than those in other districts (0.52 to 2.08) and these high indices in the three districts of the state are found even higher than those in the tropical countries like Rwanda, El Salvador, Lebanon, Haiti, Burundi, Taiwan and India where the population pressure indices range from 5.37 to 9.94 (Sharma 1998). This has exerted an immense pressure on the natural systems especially the forest resources and their products. The annual fuel wood production has been found decreasing significantly during the last decade. The per capita availability of fuel wood has decreased significantly from 0.03 to 0.013 cu m by 1997. Immediate attention is essential to check further removal of our forests and enforce plantation of trees on a massive scale through the joint effort of the concerned departments and the public.

Conclusion

In the light of the discussions made it is hightime to realise the impacts of the degradations in the land and aquatic environments. It is essential that people especially in the stress prone areas and environmentally affected regions be made aware of the causes, effects and preventive measures through environmental awareness camps, workshops, seminars etc. Success may be achieved through the sincere and tireless efforts of the public mass with full co-operation of the government.

REFERENCES

Devi, K. Indira 1998. Ecological studies of the freshwater Macrophytes in Utrapat lake, Manipur. Ph.D. Thesis, Manipur University.

Devi, N, Beenakumari 1993. Phytosociology, Primary production and nutrient status of Macrophytes of Loktak lake, Manipur. Ph.D. Thesis. Manipur University.

Devi, O. Ibeton 1993. Distribution, Primary production and nutrient status of the Macrophytic communities in Waithou lake, Manipur. Ph.D. Thesis, Manipur University.

Forest Department, Manipur 1998. Statistical Bulletin of Manipur Forests.

Forest Department, Manipur 1999. Vanamahotsava Publication.

Newman, A. 1990. Tropical Rain Forest. Eddison-Sadd, New York.
NRSA, 1990. Report on land use/land cover, Manipur state.
Ramsar Convention Bureau 1997. Ramsar information paper 1–14. IUCN, Gland, Switzerland.
Sharma, B.M. 1997. Whence the forest biodiversity? In 8th Manipur Science Congress publication. Manipur University pp. 49–62.
Sharma, B.M. 1998. Population expansion and ecological impact. In 9th Manipur Science Congress publication. Manipur University pp. 51–56.
Thomas, D.S., A.E. Launer, R.K. Switky and P.R. Ehrlich 1996. Indentifying extinction threats in F.B. Samson and F.L. Knopf (eds.). Ecosystem Management: Selected Readings pp. 53–68. Springer Verlag, New York.

Problems of Industrial Development in Manipur

N. Mohendro Singh

Industrial development is a stimulating outcome of progressive action and implies operation of principal forces that reveal the inner structure and strength of the economy. Industrialisation is therefore fundamental cornerstone of any development strategy. A perceptible change in the total level of living is in large measure influenced by the rate and type of industrial advancement. Three major considerations that reinforce the case for industrialisation are:—

— agriculture and industry link,
— structural strength, and
— modernisation.

It must be recalled that continued dependence on agriculture is a living testimony to the primitive character of the economy. Modernisation of life and tempo of living may be duly enriched through a sound process of industrialisation. Industrialisation does confer upon the economy a new vision of social interaction and economic dynamism. Therefore industrialisation has been a historical creed for any major economic aggression. As such, from time to time a new policy initiative is called for in order to meet the emerging challenges and accomodate the dynamics of the economy.

The economy of Manipur is largely influenced by the imperatives of the Fundamental Backwardness (the handicaps imposed by the geo-physical location). The extensive share of the Hill and hill areas to the extent of 90 per cent of the total geographical area suggests the necessity for a possible departure from the national strategy for development. However, till now we have been largely following the national policy although from time to time special programmes of action are undertaken for the backward sector of the economy.

Inspite of the investment in the successive plans, the manufacturing sector remains very low and it appears that there is acute problem of structural stagnation. The primary sector still accounts for 42 per cent of the Net State Domestic Product while the secondary sector only 8 per cent in 1994–95. Of course, the tertiary sector keeps on rising. Reference may be made to another economic fact that the annual compound growth rate in manufacturing sector registers a negative growth rate of 13.6 per cent at constant prices, 1980–81 during 1990–91 to 1995–96 (RBI). This discouraging state of affair is substantiated by the fact that the production value of the small scale industries records a perceptible decline from Rs. 16.18 crores in 1996–97 to Rs. 7.36 crores in 1999–2000 (Govt. of Manipur). According to a Report of the RBI (Currency and Finance Report, 1996–97) 44 per cent of the small scale units are reported sick as the units fail to make repayment of the advances for a period exceeding two and half years. These units have also the problem of erosion in the net worth due to accumulated cash losses to the extent of 50 per cent of the net value. Thus the industrial excitement in Manipur is found fairly low. In fact, it now appears that initiation needs to be made so that the industrial excitement may pick up.

Another side of the story is that Manipur has 79555 micro enterprises in 1998 of which 85 per cent are working without power and 21.13 per cent without premises (workshed). It is not a surprise that the small scale units in Manipur experience the disadvantages of shortage of power supply as a result of reported gap of 36 per cent between demand for and supply of power in Manipur. The market-interaction can hardly pick up. The state owned undertakings are not exception. The Rate of Returns in this sector is (–) 35 in 1993–94. The Foreign Direct Investment in Manipur is nil. Thus on the whole the performance in the industrial sector demands the critical examination in the right perspectives.

A few reasons can be enlisted such as:

— Lack of resource inventory of the State.
— Lack of proper policy planning.
— Limited market and capital.
— Deficiency in infrastructures and support services, limited functional unity of key departments.

— Lack of competitive production-technology.
— Limited institutional response and innovative outlook.
— Mismatch between skill development and industrial development.
— Weak social stability.

The market of the small scale and tiny products depends only on the local buyers whose preference is undergoing a change in the wake of a new trend of expansion of economic activities beyond national and state boundaries. The new temptations to buy competitive goods is, it appears, considerably fostered by the performance of the Indo-Mynmar-Border-Trade. Practically almost all the important items are allowed to come in from the third countries. All consumer durables are available at very low price.

The common problem of the infrastructural and service support is an old one. Road is bad. Transport is not available. Power is running short. Telecommunication remains disrupted. This is followed by the absence of reasonable flow of institutional finance, which has practically stopped in 1992. Another important reason could be lack of sound policy planning and follow up programmes. Till today the so called Industrial Policy of Manipur has, perhaps failed to attract the critical and time bound attention of the Government. The manufacturing sector has yet to see the commencement of its own production technology and capital market. In the light of hard facts obtaining particularly in the small scale sector where we have 5588 SSI units in March 2000 (Govt. of Manipur) five suggestions may be made to improve the performance:

1. Annual organisation of the Small Industries fair at Imphal.
2. Periodic Buyers and Sellers Meet and Market Development.
3. Time bound infrastructural and service support.
4. Review of the items agreed upon under the Indo-Mynmar-Border-Trade, keeping in view the industrial potentials of Manipur.
5. Indentificaiton of institutional linkage in the changing environment.

Regarding revival programme, the declaration of sick units based Bankers Report could be considered necessary as the Sick Unit Declaration Committee of the state is unable to finalise.

A new policy decision may be meaningfully made in the light of emerging new imperatives, new compulsions, new equations, new opportunities and new risks. The fundamental question is; *should*

Manipur go big or samll? This could be a question of sustainability of the enterprises with dynamic and competitive built-in structure. Another reality is the growing necessity for a fair flow of capital investment subsidy (25% as suggested by the Expert Group of the Planning Commission) and fiscal incentives such tax-holiday, income tax exemption and others etc. In fact these instruments have to be made "*Truly Attractive*".

Another serious concern is the deteriorating law and order situation where there is less security of life, less security of business and less security of income. The investment environment gets endangered and looks unattractive. A comprehensive Insurance Scheme for industrial units with 100 P.C. subsidy of the Central Government may be proposed.

Poverty of the family of the entrepreneur, not of the individual entrepreneur in isolation, needs to be tackled from various angles. The Group-Approach-aiming at gainful utilisation of the potential of the family may go a long way in re-establishing the industrial roots in the small open economy of Manipur.

Table 1. Some Indicators of Industrial Sector of Manipur

1.	Number of S.S.I. up to 1995–96	6177
2.	Sick S.S.I. units	2707 (44%)
3.	Compound Annual Growth Rate in Manufacturing sector at constant 1980–1981 prices (1990–91 to 1995–1996)	(–) 13.6
4.	Number of Micro Enterprises (1998) of which:	79555
	a) without power	85%
	b) without premises	21.13%
5.	Rate of Returns of the State Undertakings (1992–93)	(–) 35
6.	Ratio of fixed capital to output (1994–95)	0.8
7.	Net Value added (1994–95)	Rs. 3 crore
8.	Foreign Direct Investment	Nil.

Table 2. Expenditure on Industries and Minerals (Manipur)

Plan	Amount (Rs. Lakh)	P.C. To Total Exp.
I	0.68	0.66
II	12.08	2.02
III	35.28	2.75
Annual Plans (1966–67 to 1968–69)	18.90	2.63
IV	215.00	6.93
V	474.76	7.13
Annual plan (1978–80)	322.55	5.28
VI	3706.51	15.25
VII	7534.00	15.03
VIII	5281.11	4.31
IX (outlay)	12651	5.21

Source: Gom:- (*Directorate of Eco/Statistics, Statistical Abstracts*)

Table 3. Return of Investment (ROI)

Sl. No.	Corporation	1992–93
1.	Manipur State Road Transport Corporation	(–)90.34%
2.	Manipur Police Housing	(–)2.76%
3.	Manipur Tribal Development Corporation Ltd.	(–)98.12%
4.	Manipur Industrial Development Corporation Ltd.	(–)17.71%
5.	Manipur Plantation Crop Corporation Ltd.	(–)6.05%
6.	Manipur Film Development Corporation Ltd.	(–)43.46%
7.	Manipur Spinning Mills Corporaiton Ltd.	(–)87.67%
8.	Manipur Cycle Corporation Ltd.	(–)38.21%
9.	Manipur Cement Limited	(–)11.01%
10.	Manipur Electronic Development Corporation Ltd.	(–)50.80%
11.	Manipur Agro-Industries Corporation Ltd.	31.11%
12.	Manipur Handloom & Handicrafts Development Corporation Ltd.	(–)107.73%
	Total	(–)34.38%

Source: (Government of Manipur Planning Department, An Analysis of the performance of the State Public Sector Undertakings May, '1996).

REFERENCES

RBI: Report on Currency and Finance, 1996–97, 1997–98.

Govt. of Manipur: An Analysis of the Performance of the State Public Undertakings (1998–1999).

Govt. of Manipur, Department of Industries.

Govt. of India, Ministry of Industries. Report of the Committee on Formation of Industrial Policy for North East.

Govt. of Manipur, Directorate of Economics & Statistics, Economics Census, 1998.

Govt. of India: Handbook of Industrial Policy and Statistics, 1997.

Industrial Unit under PMRY: Micro and Macro Level Problems

Ch. Priyoranjan Singh

The paper raises some macro level issues, strategic to the success of the yojana like nature of credit flows and planned targeting of potential beneficiary. The micro level findings are based on a survey of 15 industrial units. Six units from the textile sector, 3 from the livestock sector, 3 from the mineral sector and 3 from the electronic sector were visited based upon the information gathered from these units. Five issues for discussion are raised here viz (1) Productivity, (2) Markets, (3) Raw materials, (4) Employment and (5) Management.

Viability and Status of Beneficiaries

Poultry Farm

This livestock industry is perhaps the most viable, profitable and growing industry. Raw materials being readily available and the market being a sellers market, efficient managers are able to achieve a high degree of productivity, profitability and sales growths. Efficient managers are able to spread their networks of business contacts to other parts of the country. These highly motivated entrepreneurs are diversifying their products as well as expanding their markets.

A beneficiary of the 1994–95 has been able to achieve production and sales of 15,000 kg of meat per month before the first installment of loan repayment. This is only half of his full capacity target of 3,0000 kg. The firm employs 4 people. His profits are Rs. 6–7 thousands per month. The products of this firm are directly lifted by retailers and the demand outstrips supply. He has not been able to achieve full capacity because out of the provisional sanction of Rs. 95,000 he actually received only Rs. 70,000. His workshed component was cancelled as he had one already and he thus could not achieve projected capacity. A further sum of Rs. 7000 was held back by the bank for insurance purpose. With the help of the loan he has been able to achieve a monthly growth rate of 30 p.c. in production and sales. This beneficiary has received collaborative proposals from outside firms for a hatchery firm. He also has a feed shop. In other words this beneficiary is on the verge of achieving vertical integration in this industry. At the managerial level he has problem of cash transaction at the Takyd Branch of the U.P.I. Because of this inconvenience he has not been able to make his daily transaction at the Bank. He alleges that the high hopes the bankers had given in the training programme of possible cash credits to the successful enterprises has not been fulfilled. He bitterly blames the dishonest beneficiaries whose huge liabilities to the banks is the main cause of successful firms being ignored by the banks.

Poultry Feed

From a weekly air consignment of 3,000 chicks reaching Imphal in 1990, today 20,000 chicks per week are unloaded at Imphal. The weekly sales of poultry feed at one shop in Imphal is about 100 tonnes per month. The demand for poultry feed is rapidly expanding and shortages are often experienced. A beneficiary of PMRY is selling his feeds at Rs. 6.65 per kg as against Rs. 7.00 to Rs. 8.00 per kg for Siliguri feeds sold in the local market. Even at this lower price he is able to sell only 2 to three tonnes of feed per day against an installed capacity of 10 tonnes per day. The firm employs 3 people. The beneficiary gives two reasons for lack of sales. Firstly, his firm being new is relatively unknown. He is pushing sales through personal contact. He is in the process of opening sales depot at Bishnupur, Thoubal and Kapopokpi. Asked why he does not advertise, the reply is that he may attract the 7 p.c. sales tax on feed which few other states in India impose but Manipur does. Secondly he believes that poultry farmers wrongly believe that higher cost feeds are better than lower cost ones. This firm had started only five months back. However, because of the high margins of profit this entrepreneur claims that he has paid back 12 months installments in advance. He plans to avail of cash credit to expand his production. He believes that in the long run as more firms are installed Siliguri products can be priced out of the market and feeds available in the lower prices than prevailling one. Import component of feed is 2/3 by cost and 1/3 by volume. Local production cost is claimed to range between Rs. 5 to Rs. 6 per kg which leaves a wide margin of about Rs. 1 to Rs. 2 per kg as profits. Obviously the live-stock feed sector is a potentially growth area in the State. This particular manager seems to be following proper business and entrepreneurial principles.

Textile Industries

The textile sector comprising readymade garments, tailoring, weaving, embroidery and wool knitting employ a large number of men and women in the lowest strata of society. Poorly paid and subject to exploitative cartals of traders and middle men a huge number of tailors and traditional weavers are virtually crying out for help. This sector perhaps needs greater attention of the State Government not only from the perspective of employment generation but also from the stand point of social justice. The market for cheaper and mass consumption readymade garments are virtually in the hold of a few traders. These traders supply raw materials to the household tailors and market them throughout the State. These traders would refuse to purchase garments independently supplied by the tailors. In other words the market for ready made garments are more or less closed to the unorganized tailors. Each contract tailors set Rs.1 for stiching cheap children's half pants and Rs. 6/7 for better one. Long pants are stitched for Rs. 13. Shirts are stitched for Rs. 25. Generally a master tailor gets the bulk orders and the tailors employed by him share the charges on 50:50 basis. In all cases threads, buttons, buckles and charcoal cost are borne either by the master or tailor. A household tailor with 4 to 5 family hands working 10 to 12 hours a day during peak season are able to earn Rs. 100 a day if orders are available. Surplus unemployed tailors tend to under cut the prices thereby worsening wage rates. The cost of a cheap long pant is about Rs. 75 and sells at Rs. 110 to Rs. 120 leaving a high profit margin of Rs. 35 to Rs. 45. These profit margin are however dampened by unsold stocks due to changes in tastes, fashion and income levels. It is under these monopoly situation in the market that tailor beneficiaries are to make their units viable. The entrepreneur has to develop his own distribution network, undercut prices and built up risky inventories. Only tailors with their own shops at the main bazar or indegenous marketing skills can survive. One beneficiary under PMRY, 1994–95 received a loan or Rs. 95,000. He tried to organize some fellow tailors and sold his products. He failed, lent out some money to family members and put the rest into a shop. He is back to contract tailoring. The concerned bank made no inquiry before releasing the second and third installment consisting of working capital.

The readymade garment sector which caters to the upper end of the market seems to be both viable and profitable. Readymade garment shops mostly buy their stocks at Calcutta and since price differentials are Rs. 40 to Rs. 50 per average winter price, these shops which should be classified as business and not industry seem to be both viable and profitable. One of the beneficiaries had planned of his own tailoring unit. He did not do any local sourcing as local products are costlier. The most prospective units are the producing unit. One beneficiary, a qualified fashion designer of the PMRY, 1994–95 batch has just started production. The Unit employs 6 women tailors paying Rs. 800 to Rs. 1000 per month. The unit produces high price ladies and children's wear and furnishing goods. Two bulk order inquiry are under negotiation with local traders. Traditional Indian women wears with Manipuri fabrics and designs are planned to be marketed with contacts outside Manipur. The unit will be setting up a Boutique of its own, soon. After receiving Rs. 46,000 as workshed and machinery amount only half of the working capital has been released the other half is outstanding. The incomplete disbursement of the loan has taken six months and she has received notice of loan repayment even before she has completely received her working capital. The Bank has promised to release the remaining working capital on production of wage receipts from her employees.

In the weaving sector one beneficiary of the PMRY, 1994–95 batch though she had received the full amount of the loan, she had virtually turned into a contract weaver rather than a producing and selling unit. The unit employs 7 women weavers but produces one kind of bedsheet. The raw materials are provided by the bulk traders and she receives only weaving charges of Rs. 50 per bed sheet. The entrepreneur has net daily earning of Rs. 50 only which is hardly sufficient to pay the monthly installment for Rs. 80,000 loan received. The entrepreneur has not tried to retail her own products and the traders refuse to buy her own product. Working capital received seems to have been virtually mis-utilized. In view of the market cartels only handloom weavers with diversified products and retailing skills can survive to repay bank loans. Weavers producing high quality and costly ladies wears have however greater growth, profitability and employment potentials.

The industry is highly labour intensive taking 10 days to produce one garment. Profitability is Rs. 150 to Rs. 200 per cloth. Higher the scale of production higher is the profit and employment generation. However, of the two units visited one had turned into a grocery shop and other had yet not installed the looms financed by the Banks. The second unit was however producing on the looms previously installed.

Mineral Based Industries

Utensils being a commodity with a steady and growing demand has a ready market. Lighter varieties of aluminium utensils are not yet produced in the state. Heavier cast aluminium and brass utensils employ a large number of families. This market is also a sellers market. Products are also exported by the traders outside the state. The single most restricting factor to the growth of the industry is the scarcity of the raw materials. Scrap collection and dealers being the main source, production by units depend upon flow of scraps. During peak agricultural season production is minimum. Scraps being cheaper in the state, there is a huge drain of scraps to Assam and Nagaland factories. As a result no unit is able to maintain inventories in order to rationalise sales and management. Whatever is produced is sold outright. This is a high employment intensity industry. One PMRY unit was employing 12 men with daily wages of Rs. 60, 40 and 30 according to levels of skill. He was employing only 5 men before the loan. Another unit employed 7 men at the home foundry and another 4 at a branch foundry at Kakching. Both the units had net profits of Rs. 4 to 5 thousand per month. The firms however did not maintain accounts. One established and reputed Brass and Bell Metal foundry had not yet received the first installment for machinery because the cost calculations of the original project proved to be wrong. Motivated entrepreneurs are branching out founderies to different parts of the State to escape wholesale traders and improve distribution and profits.

Electronics Industry

The electronics and electrical industry is a growth area identified in the State. Units have not been able to tap this market mainly due to the high local cost of raw materials, packaging and finish problems and high cost of maintaining business inventories. As a result some units have become near servicing units rather than producing units. One PMRY Electrical Winding Unit of the PMRY, 1993–94 batch has virtually stopped production and has become a servicing unit. The unit is five months in loan repayment arrears. The unit does not keep accounts and does not also know its monthly returns. The project profile had assumed sales of 3 welding machines at a unit price of Rs. 10,000 per month, Rs. 15,000 was to come from servicing. Cost was assumed to be Rs. 40,462 leaving a net profit of Rs. 4,538. In one whole year the unit was able to produce and sell only three welding machines instead of three per month. The market price of the machine is Rs. 16,000 while the unit sells it at Rs. 8,000 with profits. The unit does not produce and sell the machines in the markets. It produces only on direct orders. The unit cannot stock readymade machines because of lack of working capital. Because of lack of marketing skills and misuse of working capital, the unit has turned into a loss making servicing centre.

A Computer Printing firm of the PMRY, 1993–94 batch is however doing profitable business. The unit's gross income is five to seven thousand rupees and after monthly loan repayment has a net profit of Rs. 3000 to Rs. 5000 per month. The firm keeps proper accounts and shows a growth rate of 5 to 10 p.c. in business during March and October, 1995. The entrepreneur feels that the printing market is limited in Manipur and very soon as more firms are setup, only the most efficient one can survive. As such he plans to diversify his unit.

Macro Level Problems

Credit Flows

After the disbursement of the first installment consisting of workshed and or machinery costs, the disbursement of the remaining amount of the loan takes one to six months in most cases. The release of these working capital is not uniform. In some cases the working capital is released in one installment and in others in five or three installments. Firms complain that economics of scale in purchasing of raw materials and other advantages are lost. Labour costs in the early stages of productions and sales have to be met from raw material capital, further stifling productivity. Because of delays in working capital disbursements, moratoriom periods are lost while interest claims on plant and machinery accumulates. There is a need to shorten working capital disbursement period and equitability rationalizing of number of installments. Beneficiaries allege that 7 to 10 thousand rupees are held back for fire and other insurance. Some of the units got it disbursed but didn't buy the policies anyway. Such needs are better fullfiled at the beginning rather than at the last installment. There are allegation of raft against bank of officials. These allegations come mostly from those who are less educated, failing units or those who were on the verge of crossing the upper age barrier while applying. Better qualified, educated and motivated entrepreneurs said that they were not asked for draft though they claimed harrassment. These issues have even become public in local newspapers. In order to avoid such allegation there is a need for greater transperency in the final selection procedure. For example criteria for both selection and rejection could be made public.

Targeting of Potential Beneficiaries

Viability and success of a beneficiary fundamentally lies in the preliminary selection of beneficiary and target industry at the DIC level. Once the list reaches the bank, financial viability rather than economic viability would certainly be more weighted. Within the broad industrial policy priorities given to agrobased and electronic industries there is a greater need to specify a set of industries which are to be financed in each district. After these industries are specified, targets in each of them for each year and each districts needs to be set. The reason why trades like carpentry, weaving, embroidery, tailoring, iron and steel fabrication etc. have received high weightage in the State's Industrial Finance is perhaps an out come of lack of planning and targets. Further, growth in these areas can hardly be called industrial growth. There is a need to refer various consultancy reports and the project profiles prepared by the DICs to an expert committee for proper identification of industries, through targets and viability survey of some priority industries in the state needs to be carried out for the reference of the Committee.

Some of the families of the beneficiaries certainly looked much better richer than the Rs. 2,000 monthly income criterion. One beneficiary charged that one beneficiary had parents in government employment. Most beneficiaries had their own running units prior to availing of the loans. Besides possible contravention of the income criterion a vital question arises—do such beneficiaries qualify as educated unemployed as meant by PMRY. This issue needs closer examination for a better and more honest implementation of the scheme.

Raw Material Sourcing

There is a positive case for the setting up of a raw material bank. After proper targeting of specific industries, raw material and component needs of beneficiaries and non beneficiaries could be easily assessed. Bulk purchases at the sources by the Bank would definitely help local units get cheaper, better and timely supply. This bank could be a private concern with which the financing banks and State Government have close coordination in the matter of purchasing for selling of raw materials and components to beneficiaries. Working capital could then be channeled by the financing banks through this Raw Material Bank. Other modalities of organization of the Bank could be also considered.

Management and Marketing

The managerial and marketing skills of the beneficiaries are extremely low. Only a few maintain accounts, have future plans, take risks or know the various incentives given by the State Government. Units are generally integrated within the family structure physically and organizationally. Being essentially household units, impersonal profit oriented market behaviours are hardly apparent. One tends to develop a distinct feeling that separating the workplace from the family may bring about a better sense of urgency and work culture. One can also think of remodelling a suitable training programme for the beneficiary.

Population Growth: A Threat on Development in Manipur

R.K. Narendra, N. Sharat and K.K. Singh Meitei

Abstract

The article highlights the trend of population growth and its impact on the development plans with particular reference to Manipur State. The interpretation and discussion is made on the basis of secondary and tertiary sources. The finding shows that there is an urgent need of population control in the state since the population problem becomes a serious common issue on development plans in Manipur.

Introduction

Population explosion is the most ominous force in the world today. The menance is accelerating very fast and despite many steps taken up from all feasible angles to meet it, the situation is alarming. The tidal wave of population hampers all the buds of developmental plans. The MAN is the only peril to lie at the root of all problems around us. Over population and its fatal activities give a tremendous pressure on land and environment where we survive.

Human beings are intellectual creatures created by God as His Vicegerent to rule the planet. It is therefore our duty to forbid the catastrophe hovers around us. We are now at the turning point of 21st century. Whether to save human species or not from this futile earth is in our hands. Our negligence in this crucial juncture may cause the fusion population.

The crux of the matter in the present article is to highlight the population trend of the world, India and Manipur State to some extent. And a more emphasis is made to analyse the impact of population growth on the developmental plans with particular reference to Manipur State. It shows that there is a large gap between demand and production in the State by reason of the high rate of population growth and fixed rather diminishing arable land as well as limited natural resource. There is a need for better and effective developmental planning in the state that the rapid population growth in the State should be checked from all feasible angles in order to have a sustainable development especially economic in the State.

History of World Population

Man is believed to be one of the last living species linkage on this planet, Earth. According to the opinion of prehistoric archaeologists and palaeodemographers man, or a very close kin to man, has been on the face of the earth for perhaps 3 million B.C. and again separated off from the animal kingdom approximately a million years ago. The research findings make it possible to retrace an approximate picture of the dynamics of population in very ancient times. For hundreds of thousands of years during Paleolithic mankind multiplied extremely slow. At the end of the Paleolithic the figure had reached about 3 million. During the Mesolethic, the rate of population increase rose compared with the Paleolithic and touched about 15% per millennium, while the population rose from 3 to 10 million, during Neolithic, the population increase from 10 to 15 million.

The American scientist M.K. Bennett, director of the Food Research Institute of Stanford University estimated world population at 1000 A.D. 275 million. For the next far centuries he gave the estimated figures of world's population. After him, British demographer A.M. Car-Saunders and the American W.F. Willcox estimated the population in subsequent centuries upto 1900 based on circumstantial theoretical analysis. According to their estimate the population was 545 million at 1650 and 1650 million at 1990.

History tells that world population grew slowly at the very beginning and then at faster rate. It took million of years to reach the level of 230 million at the beginning of the Christian Era. It again touched 545 million in 1650 and 1 billion in 1830 A.D. The population rose from 1 billion to 2 billion in 100 years i.e. from

1830 A.D. to 1930, in the subsequent 30 years to 3 billion i.e. from 1930 to 1960 and in another 15 years to 4 billion i.e. from 1960 to 1975. Around 5 billion was achieved in only 10 years i.e., from 1975 to 1985. Now, nearly 86 million people are being added to the volume of world population per annum. A group of United Nations experts confirmed that the world population reached 6 billion on 13th October 1999. At present it is expected that the figure becomes around 6.1 billion people on the earth. In another six hundred years from now, there will be one person standing on each square feet of land on earth just like standing position in a crowded bus or a train. If the population continues to grow at the existing annual growth rate of 1.7% around 4250 A.D., the weight of the people on the earth will, more or less, be equal to the weight of the earth itself.

National Scenario

India, which comes under the category of developing countries, with the second largest population in the world, is not an exception to the situation emerging from rapidly increasing population. Once Indian population had a negative growth during the decade 1911–1921 and after that it has been accelerated very fast. For instance, the population has grown from 251 millions in 1921 to 685 millions in 1981 and 846 millions in 1991. Aastha, the second baby and daughter of Ashok Arora and Mrs. Anjana, was officially designated as the 1st billion Indian who was born at 11.40 A.M. on the 11th May 2000 with a birth weight of 3.1 kg. Now India covers 16% of the world's population on 2.4% of the globe's land area.

State Scenario

In context of Manipur, the population of the state is accelerated very fast. The population was only 284465 in 1901 to 577635 in 1951 and 1420953 in 1981 to 1,826,714 in 1991. At present the figure is projected around 26 lakhs. Among the 32 States and Union Territories of India, Manipur is 20th in rank by its only 2.5% of the National land area and it is supporting about 0.22% of the total population of India. Thus nearly every four hundred fiftieth person in the country is a Manipuri.

The growth rate of Manipur State during period 1901–1951 was more or less same as the corresponding all India rate is 12.1%

for Manipur as against 12.5% for all India. But from 1951 onwards the growth rate of Manipur has been so alarming as it is much above the National level. The decennial growth rate of the state during 1981–1991 was 28.56% as against 23.50% for all India. Their corresponding rates during 1971–81 were 32.46% (Manipur) and 24.66% (India) respectively. From 1991 to 2001, the decennial growth rate is estimated for the state as 41.9% (based on the estimated population of the State as on 1st March, 2001 will be 25,92,463). It shows that the decennial growth rate of population of the State increases. This trend of decennial growth rate again varies within the districts of Manipur.

The distribution of the population in the nine districts of the state is very much heterogenous showing a heavy concentration of population in Imphal districts. In these districts there are 707,184 persons comprising 38,71% of the total population and the second and the third positions with 15.90% and 11.33% go to Thoubal and Senapati districts respectively. One of the important features is that the average density of population in the valley comprising four districts viz., Imphal West, Imphal East, Thoubal and Bishnupur is above 16 times and average density in the five hill districts viz., Senapati, Ukhrul, Chandel, Churachandpur and Tamenglong. It may be noted that Imphal districts having the only city above one lakh population with 576 followed by the other two districts namely Thoubal and Bishnupur district with a density of 565 and 363 respectively. With 20, Tamenglong is the most thinly populated district in 1991 census.

With the cited example above, the growth rate of population in all can be treated as very high particularly in the last three decades which is the result of several attributed factors. It is a well established fact that the population growth of a country/region is dependent of mainly three components. They are fertility, mortality and migration. Among the components, migration is also one of the main causes in the state. For instance, the growth spurt after 1950 was mainly due to the removal of state's ban on immigration. According to 1951 census, 2,765 immigrants and emigrants of whom 1,687 were from Nepal, 608 from the then East Pakistan (now Bangladesh), 304 from elsewhere outside India and 166 from other states of India. The 1971 census highlighted that the immigrants and emigrants during the period 1961–71 were 11,354 and 6,313 persons respectively. Taken together, these two categories of migrations constitute 6% of the total growth in population. Out of the immigrants from other countries during the period, 2495 had their last residence in Nepal, 2381 in Myanmar (once Burma) and 901 in Pakistan and these three countries accounted for 91.5% of the total foreign emigrants. In 1976, Góvt. of Manipur recorded 95,674 persons migranted to the Manipur valley and 1,42,033 to the state as a whole. At present the over all migrated population in state is estimated to be around 3.2 lakhs. It is therefore they contributed nearly 8% of the total state population at present.

The fertility in Manipur is reported to have declined in the past decades but the population is on the increasing trend. This may be due to the sudden decline in death rate in comparison with the fertility decline, which is contributed by the advancement of health facilities and improvement of education particularly in women in the State. One more interesting feature of the state is that there is a great variation of fertility rate among the different sections of Manipur people. Research experience shows that migrated people and minority people contribute very high birth-rate in comparison with the indigenous people of the State. This factor is also one of the census which make population grown faster.

Another possible factor which may be responsible to rise the population figure of the State is that some section of the people intentionally exaggerate their population while in census for their due advantages and benefits for the governmental plans like financial loans, grant, political gains etc.

Consequences of Population Growth

In connection with the consequences of population explosion, it is a fact that a country can be developed only when it has a sound resource base with a purpose planning. Resources shrink as population increases. This is one of the major crises that for every nation facing as man is the biggest destructive agent to nature. An urgent task is thus to rectify the disequilibrium between population and resource for the well being and prosperity of the mankind. The reason is that due to increase population, the country gets into a situation where natural resources are depleted at a much faster rate than they are regenerated on one hand and on the other, all efforts of economic development goes in vain owing to the rapid population growth. Thus population control becomes a prime importance for social and economic development.

The situation is not exception in Manipur State. There will be a large gap between demand and production in the State by reason of the high rate of population growth and fixed or diminishing arable land as well as limited natural resources. For example, in spite of a massive investment in agricultural sector such as high levels of inputs as fertilizers and parasiticides and implementation of HYVs (High Yielding Varieties) in the State, the State has been suffering from food problem especially rice for a long time. It is evident that by 2000–2001 the State requires 620.37 thousands tons (based on Dandekar and Rath's norm) of rice to feed the population of the State (26 lakhs) and therefore the deficiency of rice in about 303.25 thousand tones. It is extremely feared that by 2001 A.D. around 12 lakhs people in excess will owe food population capacity in the State.

Now the State has been facing a lot of problem not only to feed their population but also sustainable socio-economic development since the tidal wave of population hampers all the buds of developmental plans. The situation will be more serious in future probably in the next decade. The only remedy to the present and future holocaust is to check the present growth rate of population and to boost up agricultural production, to some extent, in order to have sustainable development in the State.

Conclusion

One time people considered that a large population was an asset in order to have large and production labour force and a big army. Whereas today in this mechanised world, the strength of a nation is determined by its nuclear power not by its population. Excess population becomes a big burden to the nation as well as the State too. Rather population issue is a global problem and it is therefore responsible of every one. To achieve our goal of stable population in the country especially in State in order to have a sustainable development, all of us to join our hands should control population. Population control is also the best and short cut way leading to the quality of life.

REFERENCES

Berman P. The Organization of ambulatory care provision: a critical determinant of health system performance in developing countries. *Bulletin of the World Health Organisation,* 2000, 78(6).

Gargi Parsi. Spotlight on Aastha But There Were Others. *The Hindu,* Friday 12 May, 2000.

Girish Chandra. New Policy Seeks Stable Population by 2045. *Yojana,* May 2000. 5–7.

Lalita Panicker. A Billion Maternities Now. *The Times of India, Sunday, 14 May, 2000*

Narendra R.K. Population Control: Need of the Hour. *Manipur Today, Special Issue 34,* April, 1987.

—The Fate of a Manipuri. *Manipuri Today, Vol. IX(3),* 1989. 24–27.

— An Appraisal of Family Planning Programme in Manipur. *Journal of Medical Science, RIMS, Imphal Vol. 19,* 1996. 25–28.

Rajkumar R. People, Space and Economy of Manipur Valley in the Twenty First Century. *Manipur Today, Vol. IX (1),* 1989. 17–23.

The Role of Women in Manipur Politics

Prof. Ksh. Bimola Devi

When one tries to know the political position of women, one has to go deeper into the social norms, traditions and structures of the society. There is always interaction between the social norms, social beliefs and traditions and the political culture of the society. There is a gap between the social norms, beliefs and the political culture of the society or the state if the level of civilisation or development is at lower level. This gap can be narrowed down or bridged only when the political awareness, political consciousness or the political culture grows from the society itself. The gap can also be bridged or narrowed down when the people are fully conscious of their political behaviours. With this background in view, let us try to know the level of social development and its interaction with political matters in the state of Manipur since the Pre-British days and the level of political status of Manipuri women.

Women and Politics in the Pre-Historic Period

The political activities and political role of Manipuri women may be examined under two categories i.e., as an individual and as a group.

As an Individual

In ancient Manipur 33 A.D. the chief Queen named Laisana (Maharani) was a member of the council of Ministers (Mantries). She headed the women's court called 'Patcha' where all women related cases were taken up and settled. There were many women who took active part in the administration and political affairs of the state. Mention may be made of Maharani Linthoingambi who played a very significant political role in the absence of her husband in 1443. The Maharaja went for an expedition to a far place and taking advantage of his absence, the Akla tribe asserted its independence by moving its force towards Imphal, the capital of Manipur with arms. Maharani Linthoingambi after learning this, dressed up as a male person giving the look of the Maharaja and received the advancing tribe with its leader. The leader of the tribe and its force were disheartened and discouraged at the presence of the Maharaja and submitted to the authority of the Maharaja. In the night, they were given delicious meals with intoxicated material (Hidangmana) on the advice of the Maharani Linthoingambi. They were captured easily by the Manipuri force. This shows the significant political strategy of Maharani Linthoingambi. The example set by Maharani Gomti Devi also shows the high political strategy of a woman in controlling the Maharaja in the political administration of the state including succession to the throne. She wanted to take revenge against Maharaja Garibniwaz (her present husband) for killing her former husband. She made Garibniwaz to promise that her son Ajitshai should be made the Maharaja after his death though there were many older sons from other Ranis. Ajitshai was the son of her former husband though born at the palace, she was pregnant when Garibniwaz married her. Garibniwaz suffered a lot at the hands of Ajitshai and finally killed by his son. Another woman was Maharani Kumudini who after the death of her husband Gambhir Singh in 1834 pursued a policy to protect her minor son, Chandrakirti from the royal intrigues for the throne. Among the Manipuri princesses, we can cite Kuranga Nayani the daughter of Gourshyam who was married to the king of Assam. After the death of her husband, she adopted a political strategy to protect her younger brother-in-law, Laxmikant. In 1769 she killed the leader of the Maomaria revolt, Borbaruah and made her brother-in-law Laxmikant the ruler of Assam. She was successful in her political manoeuvres and Laxmikant finally became the king of Assam. Another courageous Manipuri Princess was Shija Tampha popularly known as Jandhabi Devi in Tripura, the daughter of king Bheigyachandra who had married the king of Tripura. After the death of her husband she ruled Tripura as a political head during the period from 1783–1785. She won the title of Rajmala for her able administrative qualities. Another Manipuri princess was Induprakha who married the ruler of Cachar and became Maharani from 1804 to 1831. After the death of her husband Govindchandra, she ruled Cachar efficiently and successfully. One Manipuri woman named Lilabati (Leihao) Devi took an active part in fighting against the Muslim Zamindars in a Meitei inhabited village of Bangladesh (former East Pakistan) demanding the rights of the farmers.

There were many other princesses who were married to the rulers of the neighbouring countries like Burma (Myanmar) and had played political role to protect the political integrity and sovereignty of Manipur.

As a Group

As Manipur had monarchical form of government, the common women had no room for direct participation in the political affairs of the state. But due to Lallup system (every adult male had to attend the palace service for 10 days out of 40) and frequent warfare with the neighbouring rulers and chiefs, the women had to shoulder the social responsibilities and the day to day management of household affairs. They used to discuss and interact with one another about the social and political matters in the morning or evening in the market place. This enabled them to participate indirectly in political matters of the state. They even corrected the injustice done by the king or by any officials of the state by reporting the matter to the king. They were able to postpone the scheduled programme of the king if the royal programme affects the interest of the state. This was evidently proved when Maharaja Chandrakirti Singh postponed the catching of elephant or 'Samutanba' programme upto the end of harvest.

Thus the political status of individual woman who belonged to the royal circle was quite high and for the common women, they could only influence the decision making process of the state.

Women and Politics During the British Period, 1891 to 1947

The common women of Manipur emerged as a strong political force in collective capacity during the British period. The first Nupilal, 1904 and the second Nupilal, 1939 were the notable examples. The women as a collective force was able to fight against the order of the British Superintendent asking the menfolk of Imphal to go to Kabaw to bring teakwood, bamboo etc. to rebuild the burnt house of the Assistant Superintendent. The movement was a successful one.

The second Nupilal, 1939 also marked a significant chapter in the political history of Manipur. Though the immediate cause was economic in nature, the aftermath movement had provided for a political change. It may be noted that the demand for the introduction of democratic form of government in Manipur appeared for the first time in the later part of the movement. The British also changed its policy by stopping the export of rice to other places outside Manipur.

During the British period, the ordinary common women (especially the urban market women) asserted their political rights and had given a political direction to the people of Manipur. The people of Manipur became conscious of their democratic rights and it was after the second world war that the demand for the introduction of democratic government became stronger. We may say that the political status of women in general was raised during the British period.

In 1931 there was another woman called Rani Gaidinliu who fought against the British Government. She was the leader of the socio-political and religious movement of the Zaliarongs.

Political Status of Manipuri Women During the Period 1947–1949

After Independence, the Maharaja of Manipur in response to the demand for the introduction of democratic government in Manipur adopted the Manipur State Constitution Act, 1947. The Act provided for a State Assembly to be the legislative body and the Maharaja was the constitutional head. The election of the members of the State Assembly was held in 1948. The Manipuri women enjoyed the right to vote in the election of the members of the Assembly. It was of great significance for the Manipuri women as women in other parts of the world especially in Western democratic countries like UK, women had to fight for a long time for getting their political right i.e., the right to vote. To enjoy the right to vote, there was no hurdle for the women of Manipur to fight for.

Women and Politics, 1949 to 1969

In the Parliamentary and Electoral College elections, 1952, Manipur women participated as voters and candidates. Smt. Iswari Devi, wife of late Maharaja Bodhchandra Singh contested in the Parliamentary election from the Inner Manipur Parliamentary Constituency as an independent candidate. And M.K. Binodini Devi contested from Khurai Constituency in the Electoral College election as an AMNU candidate, and got elected by defeating three rival candidates. But Iswari Devi could not get herself elected.

In 1957 Territorial Council elections, another woman Shrimati Sabi Devi, who played a very active part in the women's movement of 1939 contested as a Communist candidate from Wangkhei Kongba Constituency but was defeated.

We had female members in the Territorial Council from 1957 to 1963 and Legislative Assembly from 1963 to 1969 of Manipur by means of nomination. They were Shrimati R.K. Mukhara Devi, Akim Angnal, Lhingjaneng Gangte and A. Bimola Devi.

As collective political force women of Manipur especially of urban area played a significant role in the 1954–55 movement for the restoration of responsible Govt. in Manipur.

Women Candidates Since 1972

The number of women candidates contesting in the Assembly elections has increased after Manipur attained the full fledged Statehood in 1972. In 1972 elections, there were three candidates contesting in the Assembly elections. But all were defeated though secured a substantial number of votes. R.K. Mukhara Devi was put up by the Indian National Congress from Keishamthong Constituency and Lhingianeng Gangte also contested as a Congress candidate from the Henglep Constituency.

In the term Assembly elections, 1974, there were three women candidates. They were Lhingjaneng Gangte nominated by the Congress in Saikot Constituency, Aribam Bimola Devi, Manipur Peoples Party from Heingang Constituency and T. Kholly, an Independent in Saikot Constituency. In Saikot there were eight candidates including 2 women and seven candidates in Heingang constituency. But the three women candidates could not get themselves elected.

The number of women candidates increased in 1980 Assembly elections. There were seven women candidates in both the valley and Hill constituencies. They were:

Sl. No.	Name	Party	Constituency
1.	T. Kholly	Independent	Saikot
2.	Athing Lhinjaneng	Janata	Saikot
3.	A. Bimola Devi	Janata	Heingang
4.	R.K. Mukhara Devi	Congress	Keishamthong
5.	Kh. Bilashini Devi	Communist	Bishnupur
6.	A. Puinyabati Devi	Congress (U)	Thangmeiband
7.	W. Joymati Devi	Congress (U)	Sagolband

The percentage of votes secured by the women candidates was not very high in both the valley and the Hills. Except one, the women candidates contested against nine or ten rival candidates.

In 1984 Assembly elections, the number of women candidates was reduced to five. They were:

Sl. No.	Name	Party	Constituency
1.	Aribam Bimola Devi	Independent	Heingang
2.	Ningthoujam Shyama Devi	Independent	Lamlai
3.	W. Joymati Devi	Congress	Sagolband
4.	Ngaina Vaiphei	Independent	Jiribam
5.	Manlienniang	Independent	Churachandpur

It seems that the political parties had no confidence in the women candidates for winning the elections as there was only one woman candidate put up by the Congress. Four were all independent candidates. It may also be noted that all the five women candidates lost their security deposits.

In the 1990 Assembly elections, there were seven women candidates contesting in both the Hills and Valley constituencies. The candidates were:

Sl. No.	Name	Party	Constituency
1.	R.K. Mukhara Devi	Congress	Keishamthong
2.	Ph. Ishwari Devi	Janata Dal	Wangkhei
3.	M. Sahadev Devi	Bharatiya Janata Party	Khurai
4.	T. Ibemhal Devi	Communist Party of India	Hiyanglam
5.	Hathoi Buansing	Congress	Churachandpur
6.	B.K. Rose	Independent	Thanglon
7.	Hangmei Shaiza	Congress	Ukhrul

There was only one Independent candidate, other women candidates were put up by different political parties. The electoral performance of the women candidates was improved as three could secure more votes, though not elected. Only three lost their security deposits and one woman, Hangmei Saiza (wife of former CM Yangmasho Shaiza) was elected from Ukhrul constituency on Janata Dal ticket by defeating her four rivals. She was the first woman to be elected to the Legislative Assembly after Manipur attained Statehood in 1972.

In the by election held in the Oinam constituency after the death of the sitting MLA, K. Bira Singh, his wife K. Apabi was elected on the Congress ticket. Thus the number of women member in the Legislative Assembly of Manipur has increased to two.

In the 1995 Assembly elections, there were eleven women candidates contesting in both the hill and valley constituencies. Five were in the hill and six in the valley.

Sl. No.	Name	Party	Constituency
Hill			
1.	Chingnou	Kuki Naitonal Assembly	Churachandpur
2.	Hathoi	Indian National Congress	Churachandpur
3.	B.K. Rose	Federal Party of Manipur	Thanlon
4.	T. Kholly	National Peoples Party	Saikot
5.	T. Ngaizanem	Manipur Peoples Party	Singhat
Valley			
1.	R.K. Ongbi Sorojini Devi	Indian National Congress	Sagolband
2.	N. Manisang Devi	Janata	Konthoujam
3.	T. Ibemhal Devi	Communist Party of India	Nambol
4.	K. Apabi Devi	Indian National Congress	Oinam
5.	Y. Sakhitombi Devi	Independent	Singjamei
6.	M. Ruhini Devi	Manipur Peoples Party	Lamsang

All the women candidates except one were set up by the political parties both national and regional. But none of them got elected and some of them lost their security deposits.

In the Parliamentary elections, there were altogether four women candidates contesting from Outer Manipur and Inner Manipur Parliamentary Constituencies. They were Ishwari Devi—Inner Manipur Parliamentary Constituency in 1952, Lhingjaneng Gangte, MPP Outer Manipur Parliamentary Constituency in 1984. Anne Mangsatabam, Congress (I) Inner Manipur Parliamentary Constituency in 1996 and Kim Gangte, CPI—Outer Manipur Parliamentary Constituency in 1998. Only Kim Gangte came out successful and represents Manipur in the House of the People.

Thus the electoral performance of the women candidates is not very encouraging. The voters, especially the women voters are not fully aware of the necessity of having women representation in the decision making body of the state i.e. the Legislative Assembly of Manipur. It may be noted that in all the elections from 1952 to 1995 the number of women voters who exercised their franchise was always greater than that of the men voters. Though the social and economic status of Manipuri women is high, their political status remain low inspite of the participation of women in the local bodies as a result of the reservation provided by the 73rd and 74th Amendment Acts of the Constitution of India.

In the Assembly elections, 2000 there were altogether ten women candidates both in the Hill and Valley of Manipur. Two were in the Hills and eight in the valley.

Sl. No.	Name	Party	Constituency
Hills			
1.	Mrs. Guiliangliu Panmei	Nationalist Congress Party	Temenglong
2.	Smt. T. Ngazanem	Samata	Singhat
Valley			
1.	Y. Ratimanjuri	Nationalist Congress Party	Heingang
2.	Y. Shakhitombi	Independent	Singjamei
3.	Th. Manishang	Bharatiya Janata Party	Konthoujam
4.	A. Mirabai Devi	Indian National Congress	Patshoi
5.	W. Laima Devi	Independent	Naoriya Pakhanglakpa
6.	E. Dipta	Bharatiya Janata Party	Jiribam
7.	K. Apabi	Indian National Congress	Oinam
8.	P. Damayanti	Manipur State Congress Party	Wabagai

All the women candidates except two were put up by the political parties both national and regional. One woman candidate in the valley namely W. Leime Devi got elected by defeating her nearest rival, AK. Ibobi of Samata Party in Naoriya Pakhanglakpa Constituency. Another woman candidate in the Hill, T. Nagazanem secured second position in Singhat Constituency.

In the Outer Manipur Parliamentary Constituency, Kim Gangte was the lone woman candidate but got defeated.

Thus the performance of women candidates in both Assembly and Parliamentary elections is not very encouraging though women are recognised as active political workers and their voting turnout is higher than men. We have to wait and observe the performance of the elected women in the Assembly as well as in the local self governing institutions e.g. Panchayats and Municipalities. Their performance will greatly influence the women voters, the women political workers and the Manipuri society as a whole.

Manipuri Women in Contemporary Situation

L. Umarani Chanu and M. Jamuna Devi

When we talk about 'Manipuri Women in Contemporary Situation' it is important to discuss afresh on the various roles and hardships of women in the conflict stricken society. And it is felt that we need to understand the conflicting roles and constraints of women in a broader perspective with realistic views. Broadly, we can say that women in this part of the country is far better than their counterparts elsewhere both socially as well as economically. The history of Manipur has proved that Manipuri women can take important role in any conflicting situation, e.g. Nupi-Lal (1904 and 1939) where women fought against British colonial rulers. Women continue to participate in all the important events by taking up various roles both at the individual level as well as in groups. Various organizations are being formed to protect women's rights, to protect from social evils and to uplift the economic status. One can proudly say that renowned women groups like Meirapaibies, Naga Women Union to name a few have been doing commendable works for the society in protecting atrocities against women, protection of human rights against armed personnel. In general, women of different sections of the society have taken concerted effort to harmonize conflicts and social disorders in Manipur. However, we need to look into various aspects of their activities and constraints to analyze their roles in development more critically.

In the present situation in Manipur people are facing with many problems that cause drawback of our society. Some of the major problems in the society are; unstable law and order, insurgencies, unemployment, drugs addiction and HIV/AIDS, alcoholism, corruption, degradation of moral values, unbalanced development which is giving thrush to rural-urban migration, ethnic clash etc.

In this conflict situation women are facing various problems in different forms. Women are often forced into various unwanted or undignified professions to support theirself, children and family in general. They are compelled to take up professions like black marketing of tickets at cinema hall, flesh trade, drug paddling and other odd jobs. They are easy prey to big businessmen and employers in returns for money and security. Many women become victims like rape, widowhood, homelessness, destitution, force migration, sole earning member of the family, divorce cases, family disintegration, harassment by law enforcing authority, denial of rights to property, sexual abuse, stigma and insecurity etc. Very often, women are used as tool such as corruption and political campaign. The above factors make it difficult for women to have a secured life and think positively for further development. With limited knowledge and skills women find it difficult to cope-up with the rapid social changes.

When we talk of inequality of women status, in the concluding remark of the Beijing Conference on women in 1995, the Secretary General of United Nations said that, "There is no country in the world where women enjoy equal status as men". Whereas it is accepted that development cannot be made sustainable if men and women do not participate in every aspect. According to a United Nations Report, women perform 2/3rd of the world's work but they earn only 1/10th of the world's income. It is obvious from these facts that access of resources and benefits, control over the resources are gender biased against women and hence we should focus on women for development strategies. Gender inequality is evident in Manipur also. Women are considered as the weaker sex requiring social and economic protection. This attitude has led to a limitation on their mobility and consequent lack of opportunities for development of their personalities. Women have, therefore, lagged behind in the field of education and skill development. Literacy rate of the female population in Manipur is 47.6% whereas for that of male is 71.6% (according to 1991 census). This affects the employment opportunities for women, which in turn left them at a low status. In economic aspect though women occupy in many sectors their productivity is low. According to 1991 census in Manipur the rate of female main worker is only 15.97% as compared to 22.57% for male whereas in the marginal workers the rate of women marginal workers is 3% and only 0.5% for male. Among non-workers the rate of female is 29.86% whereas 27.95% is male. Thus women on the whole have wordless contribution in the development of the state. Women occupy in the less skilled and laborious but less rewarding job. Women have less time for education; preference is given to the male child, girl child helps mother in domestic work.

In view to the above facts there is need to enhance empowerment of women in different areas that is in education, socio-economic and political aspects. Though women are not on the better platform in the society, Manipur women are playing different roles at their best. The roles can be broadly classified into the following:

Domestic Aspect

Women irrespective of their professions have their priorities in the domestic chores. Married women are compulsorily housewives, whether they are working women, women leader, labourer or any category. Family structure in Manipur can be broadly classified into two structures viz:

(a) Joint or Extended family
(b) Nuclear family

With the change in time, the traditional joint family structure of Manipur has changed to nuclear family particularly in urban areas. But due to social change women are taking up different roles other than looking after the family and domestic chore. Very often, they are emotionally and psychologically disturbed due to differences in opinion and ideas, and responsibilities in the family management. Their home chore activities include cooking, child-rearing, collecting water, cleaning the house, collecting vegetable, child care, caring of the aged and handicapped, kitchen gardening, collecting firewood, etc. This is irrespective of whether they are working outside to earn income or just a housewife. These multiple roles of women add to the stress and tensions. Very often women are blamed if their husband is an alcoholic or drug abuser, when their son is involved in such activities, and are stigmatized in the society for no fault of theirs. Women do not have their own identity but are often identified by their husband or son.

Economic Aspects

It is significant that the women in Manipur are economically independent by engaging themselves in handloom and handicrafts, kitchen gardening, marketing of these products in the market, silk rearing and yarn making, farming, pottery, fishing and animal husbandry, pan shops, tea and snacks stall etc. Many women in the urban areas are now employed in the Government as well as private sectors, thereby, earning equally as that of men. It is disheartening to realise the fact that women are often underpaid and harassed by scrupulous moneylenders. Handloom products of Manipur has great demand all over the world. Unlike in many other parts of the country, this sector is mainly occupied by women. These products are sold in the local market as well as exported to other places and the main place where the transaction of these products are done in the women market of Manipur popularly known as IMA MARKET in Imphal. There are many constraints to the development of this industry like dependency on the outside markets for yarns, exploitation by the middlemen, low wages, lack of appropriate improved equipment, decrease in the naturally available items due to environmental changes as wood, raw materials for handloom, lack of capital for investments. Due to these constraints women are facing hardships to meet the challenges from their counterparts. Women are often termed as invisible worker with reference to their engagements in the domestic chores. Due to the unpaid economic activities women's work is not counted significant. An ILO study estimated that the value of unpaid household work constitute 25–39% of the total gross national product in a developing country.

As a part of economic role Manipuri women have cultured a traditional saving so called 'Marup' in the form of money or material. Women whether married or unmarried contribute money weekly or monthly and received their money in turns. Initially the system was based on ritual functions like Singlup (Marup for buying firewood for funeral), Chenglup (Marup for rice for saradha or din) and now it is more broaden. Unmarried women are more involved in marup for their 'Awunpot' (dowry), a customary item given by parents and relatives at the time of marriage.

Social Aspects

Manipuri women are proud of their strength of unity. An organization of local women so called 'Mierapaibi' initially called 'Nishaband' is very popular. This local organization was formed with the aim of removing alcoholism as many people, especially women in the family, suffer from the impact of the widespread use of alcohol among men. Nishaband group punish the drunkard in public and destroy liquor. As law and order situation worsened these groups are now actively involved in fighting against violation of human rights and other social evils.

Other women organizations are also involving in various activities. Number of registered body of women groups are increasing. Many women organizations are taking up many activities in different issues. To name some, the Mahila Kalyan Samity, Imphal, is running a street children home, The all Manipur Women Association is running a working women's hostel, a destitute home, and a short stay home. Macha Leima, Palace Compound, is running a girl school successfully and taking up various activities to address the issues related to women.

Political Aspects

Role of women in politics as a whole is lagging behind from those of men. In Manipur too women political leaders are limited. Before statehood only few women were nominated in the territorial assembly. And after statehood (1971 to till date, nearly three decades) only two women have been elected in the state assembly. Though Women in Manipur have been actively involved in politics very few women have won election so far. It shows that involvement of women in politics is very low. A few women have fought for election. As reservation of women seat in local bodies came into act women are encouraged to participate in politics at Panchayat and Municipal level. Honorable Minister Mrs. Leima is the first elected women minister in the state. However, the electoral behaviour in Manipur over the last many years shows that women are not likely to win election in good number.

Cultural Aspects

Art and culture of Manipur is famous all over the world. Women take vital role in enhancing the culture of Manipur. Costumes of Manipuri women varied with different occasions reflecting the cultural heritage of the state. Women participate equally with men in traditional as well as cultural activities.

Games and Sports

Though Manipur is a small state with just 1.8 million population, is well known in the field of games and sports. The indigenous games like polo, kang, yubilakpi, mukna kangjei, mukna are still enjoyed by the locals and it is also bringing fame to the state. The women in Manipur have contributed immensely in various events as evident in the 5th National Games which was held in Manipur. They won many medals both at national and international levels. Women like Kunjarani, Sanamacha Chanu, Brajeswari etc., have played at international levels. In the events like cycling, judo, hockey, weight lifting, Manipuri women have brought name for the state.

Religious Aspects

In the festivals like Lai Haraoba, holi, durga pujah and jhulon, it is common to see women singers in groups. Participation of women in religion is evident from the evidences of maibis during lai haraoba. Maibies who are believed to be communicating with the God in trance.

Health Aspects

There is clear indications of negligence of health of women due to various factors such as poverty, repeated pregnancies, lack of proper dietary habits, inaccessibility of care facilities etc. The recent increase in women affected by HIV/AIDS in Manipur has to be seen as a symptom as well as the outcome of women multiple vulnerability. Women are primarily seen in their roles as mother and wives and not as women in their own right. The status of women is identified by their parents, husband or children. Widow of drug addict or alcoholic or HIV/AIDS, patients is outcaste by the society for no fault of theirs.

There is lack of marital decision making power and lack of power over their body. There is disproportionate discrimination in the right to health as is clearly evident in the care of HIV/AIDS which is obstructing women Human Rights.

It may be concluded that, women in Manipur are facing with problems due to various reasons such as deteriorating law and order situation, poverty, unemployment, discrimination, low rate of education, lack of infrastructure for development and lack of awareness. There is need to tap the potentials and involve them in strategic planning for empowerment of women in Manipur. Thus in order to empower women we need to focus more on education, health, income generating facilities and women welfare programmes in particular.

REFERENCES

Feminism in a Traditional Society (Women of the Manipur Valley) By: Manjusri Chaki-Sircar.

Manipur Today (15th August 1990).

Stastical Handbook of Manipur (1992).

L. Umarani Chanu. Social worker, working in Loktak Development Authority. Columnist in Poknapham Daily Paper. Secy: Organisation for Women in Need (OWN).

M. Jumuna Devi. Social worker, working in Continuum Care of AIDS Project, President: Development and Empowerment of Volunteers Integration (DEVI).

Women's Movements in Manipur

Dr. Gina Shangkhàm

When we talk of the women's movements in Manipur, to the generally awared section, women's agitations of 1904 and 1939 are recalled to mind. On these well documented and so much-written historical events, I shall not dwell upon. Then comes the Meira Paibi movements in the valley which I am not so much confident and competent to speak about. I shall confine my parameters to the tribal women's movements, that too, narrowing down to the women's movement in the Naga Community.

When we talk of tribal women's movements, the Naga Women's Union, Manipur (NWUM), Zomi Mothers' Association (ZMA) and Kuki Women Union, Manipur (KWUM) are the prominent bodies which are contributing in the awareness building about the world around them,—enhancing the process of their empowerment in their own unique ways.

Let me now trod the safe path of my own confidence by narrowing down to the Naga Women's movements. Here too, we may divide them into pre-Christian and Christian periods.

In the Pre-Christian era, though there was nothing to call as movement, there was certainly an organised commune of women in the form of "*Girls' Dormitory*" housed by a respectable family in the village community. This dormitory system afforded the natural growth of leadership amongst women in the village. It is here, where the girls lived together, sat together, sang together, learned together all the arts of weaving, spinning, handicrafts, singing, dancing, processing, designing etc. The ones who could develop their talents and ingenuity to the fullest, naturally became the accepted leaders and they command respect and honour in the society (*P.A. Thekho*,

Traditional Education unpublished, 1998. p. 2). The talents developed because the elder peer groups could enforce strict discipline to the younger peer groups in the dormitory. Trained under such rigorous discipline, the girls are ushered into the real world of the responsibilities they had to own up in the life with their husbands, their in-laws and their children.

Traditionally, women have a strong hold over the economy as the more hard-working section of the society. The hard working women also enhance the social stability and harmony of the tribals. Through their hard working, lowly, patient, sincere and morally upright life, women instil the instrinsic values to their children. It is also the mother who goads the family members to participate in all social and economic activities such as cultivation, games and sports, singing, dancing, house construction, dormitory life, community working, festivals etc. the rules of which are instructed by the mothers at home as values.

In the general administration of the village and the administration of justice, even if women do not directly participate, they exert a strong indirect influence. In the event of the lack of men's leadership, women take the place. Women can also put up cases in the village Chiefs Council court and can give witness for or against any case in the court. However, under the customary dictates, women withdraw.

Except in one or two sacrifices, women take major part in performing the religious ceremonies. In all the family rites and rituals to propitiate the household deity, the ancestral spirits, the village deity or the supreme deity, mothers perform almost all the rituals. Village priests and priestess perform almost equal responsibilities. It is the responsibilities of the mothers and the grand-mothers to instill all the significant details of rites and rituals and the zeal for and essence associated with them. The children take after the mother's spirituality. The religious fervour of the women keeps knitted the social fabric of the tribal society for it is women who impart intrinsic religious values such as love and compassion, truthfulness and honesty which are imbued in the persona of Supreme Deity as perceived by the mother.

This brief backdrop of the pre-Christian period also form the basis of all the movements in present Christian period of tribal society. The only difference is that today these are manifesting in more organised and formalised way.

The coming of Christianity brought the formal education which created awareness more beneficial to emancipation of women. With the establishment of the churches, women activities became more organised and structured.

In the traditional society, the symbols and models, particularly the women, looked up to and tried to embibe the qualities, are the household deities, the village dieties, the ancestral spirits and the Supreme Deity. The Biblical figures and personalities became symbols and models in their new faith. Thus, Eve, Delila etc. became their symbols of the negative side of the human nature while Sara, Rachel, Noami, Debora, Mary etc. became symbols of positive human nature whose qualities they should embibe and model upon.

In the local church, the roles and responsibilities of women are well defined. Women society became well-structured body through which women leadership is groomed. Church life of women is leadership training all through, much leading to the empowerment of women. Their roles and contributions in the family and church and society are immense and invaluable.

Many such women bodies of the local churches form the larger body of women at the association/council/congress/parish level. Whoever can prove their competence and efficiency at the Church level or gets professional training—theological or otherwise are absorbed in the association or congress level women's bodies. Thenceforth the proven competence from amongst the association/parish can be absorbed into their convention or diocesan women's bodies at the state level.

The coming of education and the growth of church, women society also gave a great impetus to the rise and growth of organised and formalised village women society. This set in the process of awareness building, leadership growth and empowerment at the local village grassroot level. The village level women societies constitute the tribal level societies and the tribe level bodies form the state level apex bodies. This is how the Naga Women's Union, Manipur is formed and it functions, drawing its sustainence and strength right down from the village grassroot level having 15 tribe units as the constituents of the Union.

In the Process of political modernisation, economic liberalisation and educational democratisation, the society is getting more and more complexed with its growing diverse complexities confronting in everyday life. Issues such as peace, health, gender justice, inheritance right, human rights violations, education, development, social justice etc. need to be tackled with the holistic approach and a new thrush given in the current global perspective. If women were to improve their lot, they should wallow themselves in the immediate issues confronting them with a long term vision to contribute in the development of a sustainable society. It is with this view and calling, the Naga Women's Union, Manipur came into being with its 15 constituent units right down to the village grassroot.

Language Development in Manipur

Ch. Yashawanta Singh

It is accepted that India is multilingual country having various mother tongues of major and minor tongues. There are 1652 mother tongues spoken in this country according to 1981 census. Genetically all these languages belong to four language families, viz., Indo-European, Dravidian, Austro-Asiatic and Tibeto-Burman (TB) sub-family of Sino-Tibetan. However all the languages in India have shared some common linguistic features[1] due to language contact and their area convergence.[2] India's densest concentration of TB languages is found in north-east where an almost disconnected fragment of the country is nearly encircled by Bhutan, Tibet, Myanmar and Bangladesh. By comparison with most Indian states those of the north-east are small in area and low in population, but even by Indian they are high in linguistic heterogeneity.

The seven states of the north-eastern India are very rich in natural resources and is an unexplored field of TB languages also. There are many different ethnic groups speaking more than 70 TB languages excluding Assamese, Bengali and Khasi. This small region can be compared with the vast Indian sub-continent in its characteristics for having four language families; that is Khasi to the Austro-Asiatic, Assamese and Bengali to the Indo-Aryan while

---

[1] See, Ch. Yashawanta Singh 'Common Syntactic Features between Hindi and Tibeto-Burman' in *International Journal of Dravidian Linguistics*, June 1993, Trivandrum.

[2] This sharing of common features among the languages beyond the genetically related languages within a specific geographical area is known as 'Linguistic area' or 'Sprachbound'. Another widely used (according to Hock 1986, 1996), but not very 'descriptive' term is 'linguistic area'. A rarer, but more 'descrip-tive' alternative is 'convergence area'.

other languages of Arunachal Pradesh, Manipur, Nagaland, Garo of Meghalaya, Bodo, Dimasa, Rabha etc. of Assam belong to TB language. In Moreh, a small Indo-Burma border town, there are around 100 families of Tamil, coming from Burma in 1960s, which belong to the Dravidian family.

- It is said already that in the north-east there are more than 70 TB languages.[3] Of these in the state of Manipur there are officially recognised 29 different mother tongues. They are Hmar, Gangte, Paite, Thadou, Mizo, (Lushei), Ralte, Vaiphei, Purum, Simte, Kom, Zou, Anal, Aimol, Angami, Sema, Ao, Mao, Maram, Kabui, Tangkhul, Koireng, Zengmei, Rongmei, Liangmei, Maring, Koirao (Thangal), Monsang and Lamkang. Meiteiron, officially known as Manipuri, is an official state language as well as it is used as a lingua-franca among the various speech communities. Manipuri is the only TB language that has been included in the 8th schedule of Indian constitution. It has its own literature and script.

In the history of the study of Manipuri language there are two great schools. They are (a) the Manipuri Sanskrit scholars and (b) the British Missionaries. They are analysed in the following:

The Manipuri Sanskrit Scholars

In the history of the study of Manipuri language there is a group of people who were trained in Sanskrit. They are Kalachand Shastri, Nandalal Sharma, Narayan, Brajabihari, Minaketan, Dwijamani Dev Sharma etc. They started the study of Manipuri language through the eye of Sanskrit. No doubt, they had contributed a lot in the study of Manipuri language. Unlikely their approach is traditional not a scientific study. Because they refer to the set of attitudes, procedures and prescriptions characteristic of the prelinguistic era of language study and especially of the European school grammars of the 18th and 19th centuries. The emphasis on such matters correctness, linguistic purism, literary excellence, the use of Latin model and the priority of the written language characterises this approach, and is a contrast with the concern of linguistics for

[3] See K.S. Singh's article 'The Scheduled Tribes and Their Languages' in *Languages of Tribal and Indigenous Peoples of India* (ed.) by Anvita Abbi, 1997. Motilal Banarasidas.

Also see Ch. Yashawanta Singh's article 'The Tibeto-Burman Languages of North-Eastern India' in *Manipur University Reasearch Journal of Humanities and Social Sciences* (ed.) by Prof. S. Shyamkishore, Vol. 5, No. 1. 2000.

descriptive accuracy, appropriateness, criteria of analysis, comprehensiveness, explicitness, etc. It is their opinion that grammatical category[4] is universal. They used and apply Sanskrit terminology and concept.

They grossly imposed whatever Sanskrit had—concept and grammatical principles in the study of Manipuri, for example, Tense and Voice. In the same manner of Sanskrit they divide in Manipuri, tense into Present, Past and Future. Each of these (Past, Present and Future) divided into four—indefinite, continuous, perfect and perfect continuous. In Manipuri, tense is not distinctive whereas Aspect is more distinctive. It is a characteristic of TB language. Tense is a category used in the grammatical description of verbs, referring primarily to the way the grammar marks the time at which the action denoted by the verb took place. In the very short and precise words of Comrie, 'tense is grammaticalized expression of location in time' (Comrie 1985a). One can look at a particular form in a language, determine whether or not it is a grammatical category, and then pronounce it to be tense or something different. The difference between *Jack goes* and *Jack went* in English is one of tense, whereas that between *Jack Goes* and *Jack is going* is rather one of aspect.

It is an empirical claim that tense is expressed by means of grammatical categories, for instance, English, Hindi etc. It is also an empirical claim that, in fact, tense is not found in all languages (Lyons, 1968).

In some instances, the claim that a certain culture lacks a concept of time is based simply on the fact that the language in question has no grammatical device expressing location in time, i.e. has no tense. Perhaps the most famous such equivocation is in Whorf's account of Hopi, where absence of straight forward past, present and future categories, and the over-riding grammatical importance of aspect and mood is fallen to be indicative of a radically different conceptualization of time.[5]

---

[4] Constraint played on the occurrence of the word in syntactic units may be classified grammatical categories. The units of a sentence have specific constraint in relation with other units of the sentence. They are not free from one another. Semantic springs up from the constraint.

'Any of various categories distinctions within which are expressed by variations in the form of lexical or phrasal constituents.' Among the most frequently occurring grammatical categories are person, number, gender, case, tense, aspect, mood, voice, degree, and deitic position.

[5] See Caroll (1956). For through refutation of Whorf's views on Hopi tense, see Malotki (1983).

Tense is a deitic category, i.e., locates situation in time, while aspect is not concerned with relating the time of the situation to any other time point, but rather with the internal temporal constituency of the one situation. One could state the difference as one between situation—internal time (aspect) and situation—external time (tense). Tense locates the event in time while aspect characterises the internal temporal structure of the event (Chung and Timberlake 1985).

We can give favourable consideration to Sino-Tibetan linguists' opinion that tense is not distinct in TB languages. This indistinctiveness of tense is one of the structural features of the TB languages. Bauman (1975) remarks that morphologically unmarked status of tense is a feature of TB. Again Zograph (1980) remarks that tense (a relative time) is usually expressed by the addition of supplementary focussing words. The indistinctiveness of tense is seen clearly in Manipuri while aspect is more predominant in the case of Manipuri as it belongs to TB language (see for detail Yashawanta, 1995). There are four aspects in this language, i.e., simple, continuous, perfect and unrealised (irrealis).

Aspect which is very relevant and predominant in the analysis of Manipuri is not discussed by them; in lieu of it they discuss tense. They apply wrongly.

Another is the case of Voice. There is no question of voice in Manipuri. But they, the traditional grammarians with wrong notion, analysed Manipuri having three kinds of voice:—Active, Passive and Quasi-passive. They did not analyse the language scientifically. A passive cannot be recognized in terms of its noun phrases (NP) being marked or deleted or positioned in the sentence in ways different from those used in (basic) actives. The formation of passives in and language takes place at the level of verb-phrase syntax (Keenan, 1985). No language forms passive sentences by assigning a characteristic intonation contour to an active, or by inserting a sentence-level particle in an active, or by inverting the subject and the auxiliary of an active. Rather, passives are formed by deriving verb phrases in certain ways.

What is distinctive above the form of passive sentence is their VP and passive VPs are naturally expressed in the simplest case as syntactic and morphological modifications of transitive verbs(Tvs). More specifically, a passive VP in a language will consist of a strict morphological modification of a TV together with, in some languages, an auxiliary verb specific to the passive construction. The general syntactic form of passive VPs may be described by the equation.

VP + pass = {(AUX), m (TV)} where **m** is a strict morphological function

Voice is not universal. Some languages have no passives. In support of the statement, we note that many languages in New Guinea, like Enga (Li and Lang 1978) are cited as having no passives. Similarly Chadic languages are typically passiveless (Hausa being a partial exception here, see Jaggar 1981). Also passiveless are Tamang (Sino-Tibetan; Mazaudon 1976), Isthmus Zapotec (Oto-Manguean; Pickett 1960), Yidin (Australian, Dixon 1977).

The famous and very common (a) **tha u-re** '(s) have/has seen the moon' and (b) **tiki cak-le** 'charcoal burns' are not the passive sentences in Manipuri. Sentence (a) **tha u-re** is not a passive sentence; it is the deletion of subject; any person, viz., I, he or any noun viz. Tomba, Chaoba can be the subject. And sentence (b) **tiki cak-le** is an intransitive sentence. More and above, the passive rules, mentioned above, are not seen present in these two sentences. So Manipuri is a passiveless language.

There are other things also they applied wrongly in their study of Manipuri, for instance, grammatical number and gender. Manipuri has no grammatical number—singular and plural. Even though they added dual number by introducing **əni** 'two' to noun phrase, e.g. mi **əni** 'two man', əŋaŋ **əni** 'two boys'. Again they imposed wrongly 'grammatical gender' when it (grammatical gender) is not found in the language. They used the grammatical gender term viz., masculine, feminine and neuter. But Manipuri has no grammatical gender; it has only natural gender i.e, male/female. What they mentioned the examples like:—**ipa-ima, tada-ice,** are the opposite words, not the grammatical gender. In other words they are the opposite words of the natural gender. More and above, they again imposed Manipuri has grammatical gender giving Sanskrit paradigms.

devə devi

indra indrani

Besides these, they interpreted that Manipuri has preposition/ **nakən**/and relative pronoun/ə**du**/ which are not preposition and relative pronoun respectively. They also introduced many Sanskrit grammatical terms and concepts in the study of Manipur.

On the whole, what we learnt Manipuri grammer in the school days in 1960s are not exactly Manipuri grammar but are learning just like Sanskrit Manipuri grammar. From the first schooling we had started learning wrongly interpretéd grammar of Manipuri. Each and every student had learnt this. Now it is hard to make correction and to erase the stain from the minds of the people. Because more than 40 years people are trained in the same pattern. People trained in this are always against the notion of Modern linguist. This becomes a constraint in the development of Manipuri language.

In the same pattern of the Sanskrit Manipuri grammarians, the British Missionaries, namely, William Pettigrew's Manipuri Grammar (1912) and A.J. Primrose's Manipuri Grammar (1887) played the same game. It also harden the belief of the people in the understanding of Manipuri language. It creates another point of constrain in the development of Manipuri language.

Controversy of Meitei Mayek

As regard Manipuri script, locally know as Meitei Mayek, it is very controversial due to lack of scientific studies. And there are three major questions: first, when exactly it is created; secondly, whether it is an own creation or not and thirdly, how many letters are? All the answers of these questions are not satisfactory, they are not free from controversy.

For giving answers to the above first and second questions, it is very necessary to incorporate the following three different opinions:

a) The views of Britishers,
b) The views of Indian scholars (Non-local), and
c) The views of local scholars.

These are discussed below:

a) *The Views of Britishers*

The Britishers are Hudson (1975), Damant (1875), Brown (1973) and Dun (1981). Except Hudson, the three others have the same opinion. Grierson quotes—Hudson's opinion "that local tradition declares that the art of writing was acquired from Chinese who came to Manipur about 1500 A.D. This opinion is totally rejected on the basis that they (Chinese and Manipuri writings) are quite different from each other." Grierson again quotes Damant's opinion that

> "... the old Manipuri alphabet was introduced from Bengal in the reign of Charairongba, who flourished about 1700 A.D. There are no traces of the existence of writing in Manipuri before that time" (Grierson p. 21).

Brown and Dun have the same view. In the opinion of Brown "the written character of the Manipuris is a modification of the Nagari" (1873: p. 94). The same is the view of Dun. In his words 'the Manipuris possess a written character of their own, which seems a modification of the Nagari'(Dun, 1981: p. 29). Grierson endorsed to the opinion of Damant, Brown and Dun; this is substantiated by showing Manipuri script on page 2 of his (Grierson's) Linguistic Survey of India (LSI) Vol. III, Part III. But he does not express his own view.

b) *The Indian Scholar's View*

In the line of the Brisishers (i.e. Damant, Brown and Dun) the Indian scholars like S.K. Chatterjee and Bholanath Tiwari express their opinions that Manipuri script is a modified form of Devanagari or Bengali script. But they did not present appropriate evidence.

c) *Local Scholar's View*

In their views also there are two opinions: one is saying that it is their own creation and another is that it is derived from Brahmi (from Devanagari, Bengali and Assamese). The first view is supported by books, namely, Cheitharol Kumbaba (The Royal Chronicle), Wakoklon Thilel Salai, Amailon Pokok, and scholars like Padma Shree Khelchandra Singh, Shree Wangkheimayum Tomchou Singh and Meitei Mayek Expert Committee Report (1979) etc. The second view is supported by the Manipuri Sanskrit scholars, namely, Nandlal Sharma, R.K. Jhaljit Singh, Manipuri Sahitya Parishad etc. In this juncture scientific analysis and further studies are felt necessary to answer satisfactorily to these questions.

The first stone inscription in Meitei alphabet was installed by Kyamba, the Meitei King (1467–1508) at Khoibu village in south-east Manipur and the writing of Cheitharol Kumbaba also commenced during his time. These facts at least refute the categorical assertion of G.H. Damant.

The British scholars like Damant (1875) and Hudson (1975) point out that the 'Meitei' script has been developed as late as 16/17th century. On the contrary, W. Yumjao Singh, a local scholar has pushed back the date as early as 3rd century A.D. (1935: p. 19). Unfortunately there is no valid historical evidence to substantiate the view. Learning and production of Meitei manuscript were started during the reign of King Khagemba (1597–1652 A.D.) and up to the close of the 17th century, i.e. until the conversion of Hinduism. They cover as varied subject as traditional faith, mythologies, rituals, administrative codes, chronicles, geneologies, description of different hills found in Manipur and also valuable stones, study of clouds, prediction, astrology, description of nature, ballads and other imaginative works of pure literature (Manihar Singh, 1976).

An important point that emerges from the study of the manuscripts is the fact that uptil about the beginning of the 18th century they were completely free from any loan word. In fact, loan words from Sanskrit and Bengali languages particularly have been found in manuscripts produced from 1709 onwards. The findings from study of loan words in the old manuscripts lead to see the linkages between religion and script (Aggarwal, 1997). According to Sanatomba Singh (1994) in fixing the date of the creation of Meitei script, based on the inscriptions on stone, coins and written documents, Meitei script may be created as early as during the reign of King Khagemba (1579–1652), by the end of the 16th and beginning of the 17th century.

In naming the letters also different opinions are put forward—one group likes to read as Hindi, another wants to read as Bengali while another group wants to read as *Kok* for/K/,*s∂m* for/s/, *lay* for/l/etc. taking from the names of the body-parts (i.e. *kok* 'head' *s∂m* 'hair' *lay* 'forehead').

To read as of the second group: *kok*, *s∂m* etc. is more closer to the originality of its own though naming of the letters is not related to the letters (Deringer), (As Latin reads as Alpha for A, Beta for B). Or we can read as Hindi *k∂*, *kh∂* etc. or we can read as *ko*, *kho* etc. In case we read as Hindi, *k∂*, *kh∂* etc. it is easy to teach children because the naming of the sound is closer to the phonetic value of the phoneme. There is no point to create controversy among our great scholars.

Another controversy is on the number of letter: one group wants to have 35, another wants 27 and the third group wants 18.

It is the opinion of the linguists that there should only those of sounds which are and can be pronounced by the speakers, i.e. only 24 consonants and 6 vowels. There should not be only more additional phonemes to these phonemes (24 and 6). Manipuri has no retroflex sounds because we cannot pronounce. As a whole TB languages have no retroflex sounds. This controversy becomes a hurdle in the development of Manipuri language.

For reading *Puyas* there should be an additional effort for the very scholar, everybody does not have the intention for reading Puyas, only a few persons intends to read Puyas for his/her research work.

Another controversy which is becoming a constraint in the development of Manipuri language is between Meitei Mayek and Bengali script. There is a wave of revivalism: Meitei mayek wants to replace Bengali script. Because of this internal fight, Manipuri language is not inscribed in the Indian denominations. This is the result of the controversy among the Manipuri great scholars. It is the reflection of parochial outlook: there is a tendency of 'Our Mayek' and 'Their Mayek' among the groups of Meitei Mayek scholars. This is not a progressive outlook. This is not an academic exercise.

Spelling

Controversy of Manipuri spelling, we can take, as a sign of process for standardisation of the language. Manipuri written in Bengali script is facing many problems of spelling. To solve the problem the government had formed two spelling committees in 1925 and 1969.

The spelling committee of 1925 was named as 'Rules to Write Manipuri' which was very close to write of Bengali and Sanskrit. Many dissatisfactions were felt among the writers and teachers, and many complaints were made. After 44 years in 1969 a spelling committee was again formed and named as 'The spelling rules of Manipuri language', which on the whole emphasised on tone 'how to mark' and there were many number of exceptions: consistency was keeping aside. Despite the so-called modification made a great deal of confusion still exists in the spelling regulation rules. M.S. Ningomba had given criticism on the logical ground as early as 1971 (RITU 1971, Vol. 42 and 1975 Vol. 57) that there were dissatisfaction and confusion in spelling. For instance, the use of diacritic mark

(–) (under the word with falling tone) to differentiate tones in the examples given in the spelling rules 1969 No. 1 as K^g^^^^^^^^^^^^^^^^^^^^^^^^^^^^^^^^^v- Kgev; bg^^v–bgev, and Zve—Zvev should be made in the dictionary. In the same manner Rule No. 6 also states that for GKve, HKve; IKve, JKve as there is no means with which tonal differences can be marked; a diacritic mark is to be used under the word which has high tone in the dictionary. The question here is why it is to be used only in the dictionary. However, in the case of using letters B and C; D and E, no such diacritic mark is required as the first letter of each pan is being used for making level tones and latter ones for high tones. As such statements are highly confusing why can we not devise a uniform system of rules to mark the tonal differences.

One of the principles of the spelling rules No.11 was that 'words borrowed' from Sanskrit and others must be spelled according to its origin'. The continued use of the spelling of borrowed items according to their origin is a defective task. Because it is quite a burden for learners and teachers as well as to use those sounds which are non-existent in the native tongue. Therefore, sounds such as T,Q,U,V,X,W,Y,o,k,l,F,9 could be eliminated without weakening its effectiveness as an equitable orthographic expression. For instance, even though there are four sibilant sounds in writing—Q, m, 1 and k, we use only the alveolar m. Likewise the letter is being used in writing but it is never pronounced as L. Therefore, there is no point that it should be retained in writing.

Probably because of the prevailing confusion and difficulties writers and authors somehow ignore the spelling rules and they write as they wish or they think it is right. A word can be written in two or more spelling, for example:

IY kb mb
lgybv Rgybv
R'vb Mvb
FZy weZy

Not only in the loan words, the writers also take liberty in the spelling of the indigenous words, for instance:

a] Pve Pvev
b] PvEev Pvlev
c] IBev ($vBev)

Another probelm in 1969 spelling committee is the unclear concept of consonant cluster and sequence. In the spelling writing of combination of two consonant within the syllable is scientifically acceptable; in case it is not (writing of the combination of two consonants beyond the syllable) it cannot be acceptable to write in cluster. Because the two sounds uttered at a time; it cannot pronounce separately the two sounds. For instance **kwak** 'crow' **Khwaη*** 'waist' etc. Others should write in the following way:

*d^^^^g^^^^^^^^^^^v>	dgev	'to sit'
*cyb$_b$v>	cybbv	'altogether'
*jvwK$_j$>	jvKwj	'(is) coming'
*cżK$_b$v>	czKbv	'belly'
*(Pwj$_j$>	(Pjwj	'(is) running'

Inconsistency in spelling and lack of regularity in spelling create the pedagogical problem in learning as well as the pedagogical problem of teaching children. It further creates confusion among the writers and learners. It certainly happens a constraint in the process of standardisation of the language. Then it has become a constraint on the development of the language.

The 29 dialects are more or less same in the development of their studies. They are not yet fully and scientifically studied, even a primary analysis on the very dialect was not yet done. On some of the dialects scientific analysis have done. They are Maring, Tangkhul, Mao, Hmar, Paite, Mizo (Lushei), Thadou, Tarao, Moyon, Lamkang. However, the studies are not exhaustive. On a particular aspect, e.g. Word formation, Root and affixes, Verb, Negation, Imperative, Interrogation etc. exhaustive study is not done yet. Not only there are many things to be done, for instance, in the area of phonology, in the area of morphology, in the area of syntax.

There are many dialects, namely, Zou, Gangte, Simte, Koireng, Rongmei, Zengmei, Liangmei, Purum, which are not yet started studying by any scholars.

On the whole, there are many important unexplored fields of linguistics which are very important to study for establishing the relationship among the sister languages of TB. They are:

1. The sociolinguistic study of Manipuri and other 29 mother tongues.
2. The historical study of 29 mother tongues and their relations.
3. Dictionary making of Manipuri and other 29 mother tongues.

4. Comparative study of all these languages.
5. Descriptive analysis of each mother tongue/dialects.
6. Reclassification of the languages/dialects.

The study of these broad aspects will help in the understanding of the language and dialects and in the understanding of their relations among them. More and above, the study of Manipuri and these dialects may bring out challenging results to the Greenberg's Universal (1963). There is one polar linguistic situation in Manipur: that is, in Ukhrul district, people speak Tangkhul but each village has its own varieties. They are unintelligible in inter-village communication. When they communicate among themselves, they use Ukhrul standard dialect or Manipuri. Opposite to this is Churachandpur where there are Thadou, Paite, Hmar, Kom, Gangte, Simte, Zou, Vaiphei they can communicate each other. That is, Thadou speakers understand Kom, Paite, etc. and vice-versa. But still they claim they speak different mother tongue. They may be dialects of one. This is the linguistic presumption; study is needed. The study of these polar linguistic situation may bring out interesting linguistic finding.

In Manipur, on the whole, there is no proper language planning as well as there is no authority to implement, for example, the spelling regulation of 1969. The lack of language planning in Manipur, all the 29 dialects and Manipuri language are not properly looked after for development and are not (properly) planned for development.

The missionaries and the western-way of life affect the conceptualization and understanding of their language specially. They take, in one way, similar to English. This is come to know when data collection is done, specially in the collection of data on Tense.

The centre had approved the Three-Language-Formula (TLF) in August 1961. The TLF is approved by almost all states and Union Territories in principle. But how far these states and Union Territories are honest in its implementation? The answer is not satisfactory. It is found that many states except a few are not at all implementing the three language formula in its true spirit (see K. Vishwanathan, 1999 June). There is a need to evolve a more feasible and practical approach to the TLF. The mother tongue of the pupil wherever possible, or the regional language recognised by the state should be the first language; the students can be motivated to learn by giving cash incentives and by making cultural tour to the area where those languages are spoken. These have to be done by the authority as a language planning.

In case language planning is not made up in this state some dialects/languages may be extinct. There are many endangered languages/dialects in the state, namely, Tarao, Moyon, Koireng, Purum, Zou etc. In this state Chakpa was extinct. The UNESCO Courier, April, 2000 reported that 'at present 10 languages disappear every year somewhere in the world'. In Africa, more than 200 languages have fewer than 500 speakers each and may die out. The minimum number of speakers to ensure survival is put at 100,000. Crystal (Crystal, 2000) opined that though English may be the only one global language we need care other languages also on the ground (I) we need diversity, (ii) languages express identity, (iii) languages are repositories of history, (iv) languages contribute to the sum of human knowledge and (v) languages are interesting in themselves.

Language planning and implementation have to go together for the development. The speakers are emotionally attached to their mother tongues and their literature. There is an urgent need to develop. All the 29 dialects should be learnt upto, at least, primary level. Any language should not be imposed to be learnt by others. Motivation should be created to learn. In a multilingual society proper language planning is necessary.

REFERENCES

Aggarwal, K.S. 1997. 'Script and Ethnolinguistic Identity: The Meiteilon Quagmare'. In *Languages of Tribal and Indigenous People of India*, edited by Anvita Abbi, Motilal Banarasidas, Delhi.

Bauman, J. John, 1975. Pronoun and Pronominal Morphology in Tibeto-Burman. Unpublished, University of California, Berkeley.

Brown, R. 1824. Statistical Account of Manipur. 1st Publication, Calcutta.

Chung, Sandra and Alan Timbelake, 1985. Tense, aspect and mood. In Timothy Shopen (ed.), *Language Typology and Syntactic Descritption*, Vol III. Cambridge: Cambridge University Press. pp. 202–258.

Comrie, Bernard, 1985a. Tense. Cambridge: Cambridge University Press.

———, 1985b, Aspect. Cambridge: Cambridge University Press.

Crystal, David, 2000. Long Death. Cambridge: Cambridge University Press.

Damant, G.H. 1975. 'Specimen of Manipuri Alphabet'. In *Proceedings of Asiatic Society of Bengal* (ASB), Calcutta.

Dun, E.W. 1981. Gazetter of Manipur, Delhi.

Greenberg, J.H. 1963. 'Some Universals of Grammar with Particular Reference to the Order of Meaning Elements'. In Greenberg (ed.) *Universals of Human Language*, Cambridge.

Grierson, G.A. 1904. Linguistic Survey of India, Vol. III, Part III. Ist Edition, Motilal Banarasidas, Delhi.

Hudson, T.C. 1975. The Meithei. Neeraj Publishing (Reprint), New Delhi.

Keenan, Edward, 1985. Passive in the world's languages. In Timothy Shopen (ed.), *Language Typology and Syntactic Description*. Vol. I, Cambridge University Press.

Matisoff, James A. 1994. 'Regularity and Variation in Sino-Tibetan'. In *Current Issues in Sino-Tibetan Linguistics*. Ed. Hajime Kitamura et al. Osaka, Japan.

Primrose, A.J. 1987. Manipuri Grammar, Govt. Press.

Pettigrew, William 1912. Manipuri Grammar. Pioneer Press, Allahbad.

Vishwanathan, K. 1999. 'An Anatomy of three language formula. In *International Journal of Dravidian Linguistics*, Vol. 28: 2, June.

Yashawanta Singh, Ch. 2000. The Tibeto-Burman Languages of North-Eastern India. In *Manipur University Research Journal of Humanities and Social Science*. Edited by Prof. S. Shyamkishore Singh Vol. 5, No. 1.

———, 1995. The Linguistic situation in Manipur. In James A. Matisoff (ed.) *Journal of Linguistic of Tibeto-Burman Area*, Spring, 1995, vol. 18:1. University of California.

———, 1993. Common Syntactic Features between Hindi and Tibeto-Burman. *International Journal of Dravidian Linguistics* (IJDL). June 1993, Trivandrum.

Zograph, G.A. 1980. Languages of South Asia: A Guide. Longman, London.

Recommendation of the Workshop

The following recommendations were adopted at the end of the Seminar and the same has been sent to the Government of Manipur:

1. It is felt that there has been a wide gap between the people of mainland India and the Northeastern region, particularly Manipur regarding their identity. To help bridge/narrow down this gap, it is considered necessary for the mainland people to learn more about this region and Manipur. In view of this, it is recommended that a subject on Northeast should be incorporated in the syllabus/curriculum of the educational institutions/universities in the States of mainland India.
2. Manipuri language, since its inclusion in the 8th Schedule of the Constitution of India, is gradually developing. But the pace of development of this language is still very slow which calls for faster development so that it could achieve its proper form of its own. It is, therefore, considered very necessary to have an ultra-modern language lab to facilitate research works on the language. For this purpose, equipping it with modern infrastructure may strengthen the language lab at Manipur University.
3. To ensure sustainable use of the natural resources as well as human resources available in Manipur in its development, new technologies like GIS must be used in development planning.

   Attention must also be given to protect, preserve and rejuvenate the fast degrading natural resources of the State, particularly water and forest resources.
4. In order to solve the problem of insurgency in a peaceful manner, a more extensive research and new approach to find out the root causes behind the emergence of insurgency is immediately called for.

5. Regarding industrial development, it must be ensured that Development Policy Planning be made taking into consideration the regional and global imperatives. Proper operational planning like Long Term Master Production Plan, Business Development Plan, Internal Quality Improvement Plans etc. are also required.

   There is also the need for "strong political will" and "the urge to work" both at the administrative and people's level. For industrialization of Hill areas, institutional approach will be helpful.

   The present reality demands a sound optimization exercise with a strong focus on checking willful leakages.

   For a new economic and social order in Manipur, peace and stability is a pre-requisite.

6. On drug abuse and HIV/AIDS, opening of religious instructions in the medical institutions/hospitals in the state are highly suggested as it is generally (including medical science) believed now that spiritual awakening is quite helpful/possibly helpful in the prevention of drug abuse etc. Change of food habit to vegetarian diets particularly fruits must be encouraged.

   Setting up of more recreational centres, such as, parks, gardens etc. to divert the mind of the young people, especially the adolescent is immediately called for. This is to redirect their mind from indulging in unhealthy activities.

   Production of more low cost documentary and clean AD films/ short films, pertaining the realities of the problem is also necessary for mass awareness.